Universal Mind Revealed

A KABBALISTIC RENDERING OF
WHAT CONSTITUTES THE UNIVERSAL MIND,
HOW ITS POWERS WERE DEVELOPED,
AND HOW THEY WERE ENDOWED TO
THE HUMAN SOUL FOR ITS EXALTATION,

Being an Interpretation of the Secret Teachings
of the Royal Priesthood of the Egyptians

By

Edna E. Craven, DC, CTN, BCI

BALBOA.
PRESS
A DIVISION OF HAY HOUSE

Inquiries should be addressed to:
Edna E. Craven, DC, CTN, BCI
dreecraven@att.net

Balboa Press books may be ordered through booksellers or by contacting:

Balboa Press
A Division of Hay House
1663 Liberty Drive
Bloomington, IN 47403
www.balboapress.com
1 (877) 407-4847

Cover page art is designed by Edna E. Craven, DC, CTN, BCI.
Cover page 3D rendering is by Stephanie Troop.
All illustrations are by Edna E. Craven, DC, CTN, BCI.

Printed in the United States of America.

ISBN: 978-1-4525-1945-6 (sc)
ISBN: 978-1-4525-1947-0 (hc)
ISBN: 978-1-4525-1946-3 (e)

Library of Congress Control Number: 2014914284

Balboa Press rev. date: 2/23/2015

This book is dedicated to evolving
humanity: "The Unfolding Rose"

The Unfolding Rose

The rose has been frequently employed in mystical, theological, kabbalistic, and emblematic literature. "The Rose is a Yonic symbol (the supreme female energy of nature) associated with generation, fecundity, and purity" (Manly P. Hall, *The Secret Teachings of All Ages*). Exoterically, it represents evolution. "The fact that flowers blossom by unfolding has caused them to be chosen as symbolic of spiritual unfoldment" (ibid.).

The partially opened rose depicted in the dedication page is used to represent humanity's gradual growth in knowledge, which is never fully developed but is always in the process of developing. As knowledge gained by experience and study is added, the functioning of humanity increases. Step by step, humanity emerges into objective activity of qualities and faculties that have been previously involved in darkness or obscurity. The growth and evolution of humanity, therefore, is due to the increasing activity of the potential powers within it. With increased knowledge the mind is illumined, and with illumination understanding is established. Knowledge then, brings powers to their possessors, provides skills, and can fully unfold the rose.

The ageless wisdom of the Egyptians given in this book is employed to connote truths that aid humanity in its evolutionary processes. By becoming acquainted with the universal mind and its faculties, humanity can attain mastery over the purely human nature and can possess knowledge and powers commensurate with lofty evolutionary stature.

The thesis of this book is that power-bestowing knowledge has continually been partially hidden under a veil of allegory and symbol.

The atmosphere of mystery and secrecy was necessary in former times to perplex and discourage the insincere individual and to keep the curiosity seeker from discovering things that he should not discover. Moreover, this power-bestowing knowledge can impart theurgic, hypnotic, and other kinds of powers susceptible to misapplication; that is, it can bestow the power to perform supernatural things and can abnormally induce the mind by artificial means to control the person affected entirely, in both thought and action. It can also abnormally induce the mind by the will or command of another, and it can confer other abilities capable of being abused or misused.

Nevertheless, when properly used, knowledge can be of great value to humanity. Since we are in a period when many are seeking profoundly for a philosophy of life or a universal science aimed at explaining the phenomena of the universe and helping them remain faithful and strong in their hour of suffering, trial, and tribulation, the time has come when the veil may be lifted. The kabbalistic expositions of Genesis 5 (in the Christian Bible) given in this book are based upon these convictions.

Mystic Rose

Ageless, timeless, the Mystic Rose stands
In mists of wisdom and knowledge
Awaiting those who seek
Those who listen
Those whose vision draw them to the
innermost folds of the Rose.
With pulsating petals of love
She begins to unfold
Laying open for view and contemplation
Knowledge of your mind
Knowledge of your soul
Knowledge of who you are
Where you came from
Where you are going
Leading you to the sublime
When in full bloom

Kay Little

EPIGRAPH

"*Universal Mind Revealed* by Edna Craven is one of my favorite reads and a true contribution to all of humanity. This book sheds light on commonly misperceived ideas held by all peoples from all nations. The practical application portion contained in each chapter gives me the tools I need to fully grasp each concept and how I can use it in my daily life and thought patterns. I would recommend this book to anyone seeking a deeper meaning to life and how to live!"

Adam Siwwi
Frisco, Texas

CONTENTS

ILLUSTRATIONS

FOREWORD

Today, the world is changing at a faster pace than at any previous time in the recorded history of mankind. Human beings are struggling to understand why the political, economic, educational, religious, and social systems—and frankly, life in general—all seem to be in disarray. Hurricanes, tornados, rampaging fires, tsunamis, floods, snowstorms, droughts, and unprecedented weather patterns seem to be occurring with greater frequency all over our planet. Scientists, government experts, and countless others are providing the best answers they can in accord with their human reasoning, logic, and experiences. Even the things that happen to us in our day-to-day lives—accidents, injuries, breakup of friendships, and a seemingly endless list of questions dealing with our experiences as human beings—seem to defy explanation. All these can be considered mysteries of life in this world. Why? Where are the answers?

Turning to the Bible is an obvious choice. Bible readers are told to get understanding, knowledge, and wisdom. Answers to life's questions are not necessarily obvious from just reading the Bible from Genesis through Revelation. My experience has been that real understanding, knowledge, and wisdom are given through study and meditation. How many of us are willing to even spend ten minutes a day in silence, asking and expecting answers from God? In our hurry-up, have-to-have-it-now mentality, are we too busy planning our lives and worrying about what might happen (the "what-if's") to listen to or to hear the guidance that comes from within to help us in our lives?

If we cannot sit in silence to receive the guidance from within, we can at least acquire guidance by reading uplifting books. I find *Universal Mind Revealed* to be one of these books. This book contains knowledge that will help us in our struggle to know the answers to life's questions.

I have known Dr. Edna Craven, the author of *Universal Mind Revealed*, for many years and have been the recipient of her outstanding health care. Her willingness to help me raise my health to a higher level has surpassed the common and ordinary.

Throughout the years of knowing Dr. Craven, I have enjoyed listening to her words of wisdom. She has shared her involvement with the Ancient Mystical Order Rosae Crucis (AMORC), and Kabbalah. This sparked my interest, because I am Jewish and grew up learning these things.

Dr. Craven's love for God is evident. Her quest for expanded higher consciousness has culminated in the writing of this book, *Universal Mind Revealed*. Dr. Craven shared with me that the writing of this book has been difficult yet joyous. I feel that God, the Father, has blessed Dr. Craven with inspiration, knowledge, understanding, and the wisdom of the Ancient Egyptian Mysteries. She is aggressive and persistent in pursuit of the concealed answers. I know it did not come easy. She raised a family and built and maintained a holistic chiropractic wellness practice while devoting incalculable numbers of hours to the personal study of esoteric books and Kabbalah.

Dr. Craven was inspired to write an exposition to explain in detail all of Genesis 5 from Adam to Noah. This is the first time any author is making available to the general public this meticulous explanation of what the names and numbers in chapter 5 mean, not only in their verse context but in the way the names and numbers relate to each other.

This exposition is not only unique, but it is unprecedented in written form. This sacred knowledge was previously considered secret and was limited to the initiates and adepts of the mystery schools of ancient Egypt and other mystery schools that followed. I perceive that God is allowing the sacred material in Genesis 5 to be released at this time because planet Earth and its human population are evolving into higher consciousness. Therefore, it is appropriate that more knowledge and understanding be made available to the truth seeker. A casual reading of this book will give one the gist of the detailed information. The truth seeker will make the effort to go deeper and find profound spiritual truths.

I was raised in a Jewish home with both of my parents from a Jewish lineage. We were members of a synagogue in my hometown of Buffalo, New York, where I was expected to become a "Son of the Commandment" by participating in a "Bar Mitzvah" at the age of thirteen. In preparation for my Bar Mitzvah, I was required to attend a Hebrew school held in the synagogue classroom twice a week for approximately one year prior to the formal ritual. Little did I realize at the time that this Hebrew study was laying a foundation for my study of Kabbalah some fifty years in the future.

Each time I attended a Bar Mitzvah, the congregation sang a closing song, which struck my heart in a very meaningful way. Later, I understood that these were spiritual experiences. This song was another piece that would keep me connected to God and eventually steer me toward the original Mosaic Kabbalah. *Universal Mind Revealed* strikes my heart in the same way that the closing song of the congregation did. This book is an incredible blessing for me. It fueled my desire to understand the deeper figurative and hieroglyphic meanings of Genesis 5. I quickly realized that there is profound knowledge in this book. It is so much more than a collection of names and numbers that one might easily skip over when reading the King James Version of the Bible.

Dr. Craven's book is based on the original Hebrew text that was written by Moses and called *Kabbalah*. The rabbis teach a form of Jewish mysticism called Kabbalah, and their interpretation of the meanings of the Hebrew text is very different, but I am positive that there are rabbis or Jewish Kabbalists who will see the profound esoteric knowledge in this book and discover relationships between what Dr. Craven has written and the teachings and writings of the Jewish Kabbalists. The two apparently diverse mystical interpretations could be merged, resulting in higher understanding of the Mosaic wisdom that has been hidden for thousands of years.

I am a former member of Aleph Zakik Aleph (AZA), a fraternity dedicated to Jewish life, community service, and social action. Currently, I am an initiate of the Ancient Mystical Order Rosae Crucis, and I am involved in learning the deeper knowledge revealed by the Kabbalah.

I attended and graduated from the State University of New York at Buffalo. During my four years at the university, I was a member of the Air Force Reserve Officers Training Corps (AFROTC), Department of Aerospace Studies. During this time, I was also a member of the Chennault Drill Society, was promoted to the rank of cadet colonel, and received the University's National Sojourner's Medal for outstanding initiative, accomplishment, and devotion to duty. In my senior year, I was the director of administrative services.

Immediately after graduation, I was commissioned a second lieutenant in the United States Air Force and was sent overseas to Cigli Air Base in Turkey for my first active duty assignment. Bergstrom Air Force Base in Austin, Texas, was my second assignment. Next, I was stationed in Addis Ababa, Ethiopia. My last assignment was at Andrews Air Force Base in Maryland, where I supervised twelve people. I left air force active duty after nine years of honorable service and joined the air force reserve, where I was promoted to major. Subsequently, my path led me to pursue a career fabricating ophthalmic eyewear.

Finally, I joined the Army and Air Force Exchange Service (AAFES), where for twenty-one years I managed AAFES' worldwide optical dispensary program as well as other global service programs. My credentials include the American Board of Opticianry Certification (ABOC) and the National Academy of Opticianry of which I am an academy fellow member.

Dr. Craven, thank you for allowing me to contribute this foreword to this historic book. I shall always be grateful to have participated in your vision of helping to raise the spiritual consciousness of humanity. I am honored that we are friends, and I am humbled that you have helped me in so many ways—physically, spiritually, mentally, and emotionally.

—Robert K. Krauth, Cedar Hill, Texas

PREFACE

My aim is to show what the original Hebrew text and other referenced works actually say, and teach about chapter 5 of the Genesis account. The Hebraic method of interpreting chapter 5 reveals how the faculties of the universal mind were developed and how they were endowed to the human soul for the benefit of mankind. The knowledge given in this book is designed to aid evolving man to step out and move ahead of the masses as a pioneer and leader in matters of spiritual, mental, and inner unfoldment.

What prompted me to write this book was an inner calling, the inner voice that offered me an avenue of service commensurate with my ability, my time, and my interests. My involvement in esoteric teachings began in 1968 when I became a member of the Ancient Mystical Order Rosae Crucis, or AMORC—also known as the Rosicrucian Order, a fraternal, nonreligious, nonprofit organization—and began my studies in mysticism and arcane science. My association with AMORC laid the foundation to understanding higher knowledge of many disciplines, principally the ancient teachings of the royal priesthood of the Egyptians (Kabbalah). The combined knowledge of these teachings afforded me an advantage, which I utilized to unveil the underlying meaning of the Genesis 5 account.

Producing this book was a laborious and joyous process that took uncounted hours, during which I consulted many resources: *Holy Bible King James Version, The Hebraic Tongue Restored* by Fabre d'Olivet (FD'O), *The Unknown God* by F. J. Mayers (FJM), *Hidden Wisdom in the Holy Bible* by Geoffrey Hodson (GH), *Dictionary of All Scriptures and Myth* by G. A. Gaskell (GAG), *The Secret Teachings of All Ages* by Manly P. Hall (MPH), *The Etheric Double and Allied Phenomena 1925* by Major Arthur E. Powell, *Conceptual Physics* by Paul G. Hewitt, *Your Body's Many Cries for Water* by F. Batmanghelidj, MD, *Super Brain* by Deepak Chopra, MD, and Rudolph E. Tanzi, PhD, *Strong's Exhaustive Concordance of the Bible* by James Strong, LLD, STD, *Gesenius' Hebrew-Chaldee Lexicon to the Old Testament* by H. W. F. Gesenius, and *Webster's Unabridged Dictionary* (1946).

The *Holy Bible King James Version* was used to extract the verses in Genesis 5, and certain passages showing resemblances among circumstances. Finding the underlying meaning of the verses necessitated the use of the radical vocabulary (a series of Hebraic roots) furnished in *The Hebraic Tongue Restored*. I used *Strong's Concordance* to provide the key numbers corresponding to the words used in the verses of Genesis 5, which connected me to the Hebrew root-words and the regular meanings attached to them. Gesenius' *Lexicon* offered additional details not found in Strong's. The *Dictionary of All Scriptures and Myth* and *Hidden Wisdom in the Holy Bible* were instrumental in providing the symbolic meanings of words, names, and numbers given in Genesis 5.

The Unknown God shed light on some of the hard-to-grasp Hebrew root-words, but my use of this book was limited because *The Unknown God* is primarily concerned with the first three chapters of Genesis. *The Secret Teachings of All Ages* expanded on the symbolic meanings of some words and terms. *The Etheric Double and Allied Phenomena 1925* was instrumental in providing information on the perfect duplicate and finer counterpart of the physical body.

Conceptual Physics helped to explain the phenomenon of atoms' attraction for each other, and the nature of centripetal/centrifugal forces. In a practical application, I referenced *Super Brain* when explaining how to rid the brain of mental fug. In another practical application, I referred to *Your Body's Many Cries for Water* to explain the life-giving properties of water, and I used *Webster's Unabridged Dictionary* (1946) to elaborate on the meanings of words.

There is a significance attached to using *Webster's Unabridged Dictionary* published between 1940 and 1950. Unfortunately, modern unabridged dictionaries have omitted or changed word definitions or usage and therefore cannot reflect all true meanings. For example, in *Webster's Unabridged Dictionary* published in 1946, the noun *universal* is defined this way: "in philosophy, a general notion or idea; that which by its nature is fit to be predicated of many; that which by its nature has a fitness or capacity to be in many." In modern editions, this definition is omitted.

It is my hope that this book will bring the ageless, accumulated knowledge of the Egyptians to all seekers who find spiritual sustenance in esoteric teachings and to those thinkers who are discontented with the many conflicting doctrines and expositions of both Christian and rationalist teachers and writers of modern times regarding the universal mind, its powers, and the endowments of the soul. This introduction of facts and their explanation should bring peace of mind and freedom to seekers of truth who doubt conventional contradictory thinking.

Since this ancient esoteric knowledge may be strange and new to many readers—as it is in itself rather abstruse—pains have been taken to present this rendering in a manner as clearly defined as possible. The meaning of some Hebrew key names and numbers, themes and ideas are repeated in sequence throughout the book (with slight modifications to convey the periodic development of new faculties and their similitudes) in the same way they are repeated throughout the verses in Chapter 5 of the Genesis account.

Each chapter presents the verse to be analyzed in three formats. The first line is written as interpreted by the translators of the King James Version of the Bible. The second line is the literal English translation as it appears in *The Hebraic Tongue Restored* and as proven by its radical analysis and comparison with the analogous words in Samaritan, Chaldaic, Syriac, Arabic, or Greek. The third line is the transliterated form from the original Hebraic text. After painstakingly analyzing each transliterated word, the figurative and hieroglyphic interpretation was extracted. These reveal how the faculties of the universal mind ("progenies of the Adam") were developed and how humanity made in the image of the universal mind has been endowed with these faculties.

The abbreviated names of the various authors of works consulted in the preparation of this book appear at the ends of quotations and paraphrased statements. The titles of their corresponding books are found in a bibliography at the end of this book.

May this rendering bring restoration to systems of erroneous teachings so that fresh *life* may come into all spiritual activity, so that renovated *confidence* may assure many doubt-haunted minds, so that renewed *hope* may enter many discouraged hearts, and so that new *love* may arise from knowing.

SYMBOLISM: THE LANGUAGE OF THE SOUL

The Inverted Triangle

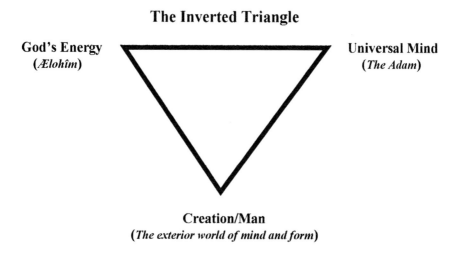

God's Energy
(*Ælohîm*)

Universal Mind
(*The Adam*)

Creation/Man
(*The exterior world of mind and form*)

The inverted triangle used on the cover of this book portrays the materialization of Ælohîm's[1] power and intelligence. It symbolizes the energy of Ælohîm focalized on the universal mind to carry out a great plan of bringing into existence beings that are to evolve in his likeness—mankind!

The twelve-pointed star inside the triangle, as depicted on the cover of this book, is a decagon. It is used herewith to signify completeness in relation to a *state of being*: man fully evolved, man spiritually perfected and complete, and man intimately connected with God.

The fully opened rose in the center of the twelve-pointed star, as portrayed on the cover of this book, symbolizes man *perfected* and man *spiritually unfolded.* It signifies that man has trod "the way of holiness" (Isaiah 35:8) and the pathway of discipleship[2] and initiation[3] and has earned admission into the superhuman kingdom.

Esoterically, the fully opened rose, the twelve-pointed star, and the triangle, portrayed in unison on the cover of this book, are used herewith to signify the *unfolded soul personality* having attained perfection by means of lessons learned and the receipt of the necessary guidance and training that aided its passage through the phases of life while on the spiritual path. The image signifies the material, physical, and earthly labors of life endured, labors that were necessary for the unfoldment of the soul. It represents the process of evolution accomplished through the soul's divine life and supplemented by the love-energy (symbolized by the red color in the rose) responding from above to its aspirations below. It expresses the culminating point of the soul personality and the soul's liberation from the *Wheel of Necessity.*[4]

The gold-colored rim on the inverted triangle and on the twelve-pointed star represents spiritual qualities to which man is to aspire: *divine wisdom* and *celestial truth.* These are endowments of the soul and are considered the *treasures in heaven* that are available to those possessing higher consciousness.

The blue color—as depicted in the two triangles composing the twelve-pointed star and the inverted triangle enclosing the star—is used herewith to symbolize "the higher mental plane and the philosophic mind and intellect" (GAG, p. 116). It portrays man's development being "directed by conscious, experienced, and continually experiencing intelligence, which is ever seeking to eliminate the rudimentary and imperfect" (ibid. 256) for "the gradual taking on of Godhead by means of the passage through matter: a returning to God full, concrete and concentric, of that which went forth from God empty, discrete, and scattered" (ibid. 257).

The white color in the two triangles composing the twelve-pointed star is herewith used to represent perfect purity, freedom from admixture with extraneous or superfluous matter, and the external nature untainted as the internal. It represents the spirit of good shining within and without man.

The significance of symbolism has always been an effort to illustrate principles and ideas. Symbols are always substitutes for the real thing, and they may easily be discarded when better ways of describing principles are found. Symbols themselves have no intrinsic power or meaning; they simply represent something else.

---

[1]   Refer to footnote 3 in chapter 1.

[2]   The pathway of discipleship refers to the disciplined qualities that are attached to ideals and from which the aspirant receives inspiration and guidance. Some of these qualities are expressed in the analytical lower mind—in faith and seeking knowledge; in expectation and advancement; in love and philosophy; in courage and forcefulness; in perseverance and steadfastness; in the truth-seeking of the Higher Mind; in chastity and receptiveness; in tenderness and heedfulness; in liberality; in discernment; and in prudence.

[3]   Initiation is a process that begins the ascent of consciousness and includes the giving of knowledge and the realization of a new power. The initiate is prepared through long periods of instruction, testing, and trial and is known historically as the *catechumen* or *learner.*

[4]   *Wheel of Necessity* is the periodic descent of the soul into incarnation, and the ascent therefrom. Wheel of Necessity is also known as Wheels of Birth and Death. (GAG, 812)

ACKNOWLEDGMENTS

My deepest gratitude goes to:

My beloved friend Thomas A. Lisemby III for introducing me to Kabbalah, the oral transmission of the secret teachings of the royal priesthood of the Egyptians. His teachings have been valuable in helping me understand what the Hebrew text actually says and teaches regarding one of the most misunderstood books ever written, the book of Genesis.

The Ancient Mystical Order Rosae Crucis (AMORC) for their teachings, which gave me a philosophy of life—a path to confident living, and laid the foundation to my understanding of advanced esoteric knowledge.

My editor and dearest friend, Lillie White. Her background in teaching and her involvement in Toastmasters International, the Rosicrucian Order, and Kabbalah teachings made it possible for her to be a great advocate in making my rendering of this book easier to understand. That is, she helped me to bring forth kabbalistic teachings in a format that can be understood by many, not just the highly intellectual or advanced student of esoteric knowledge.

My dear friend and benefactor Robert K. Krauth for his inspirational foreword, for his valued assistance in editing some of my work, and for his financial support.

My dear friend Kay Little for "Mystic Rose," her poetic interpretation of the unfolding rose, which is used in this book as a symbol for the unfolding mind of humanity.

My valued friend Yolanda Edmondson for taking the time to read parts of this book and for voicing constructive criticism.

INTRODUCTION

In his struggle to know himself, man searches for a philosophy of life or a universal science aimed at explaining who is he, where he comes from, why is he here, and where is he going. As a being endowed with intelligence, man knows that he has the power to reason, will, and make choices. To man, these faculties are evidences of his true relationship to the universal powers about him.

Further, man understands that he can harness universal forces, attune himself with them, and alter or control their ultimate effect upon him. For instance, he can arrange the affairs of his life so that he can use the forces of life as an ally. Like the captain of a ship turning his sails to the wind, like a dynamo transforming mechanical energy into electromotive force, or like nuclear fission heating water for power, man can harness the other forces of his existence. But few understand and use them. Man cannot use the powers he possesses if he does not understand them or does not know he possesses them. This book is an attempt to explain unique truths I learned about man's powers and the reason for his being.

My spiritual learning began in 1968 when I joined the Ancient Mystical Order Rosae Crucis, or AMORC (a fraternal, nonreligious, nonprofit organization, also known as the Rosicrucian Order) to receive mystical truth aimed at helping me in my quest for personal mastery.

My association with AMORC laid a sturdy spiritual foundation that enabled me to understand higher knowledge of various disciplines, principally those taught by the ancient royal priesthood of the Egyptians (the original Kabbalah as written by Moses). These ancient kabbalistic teachings I found to be rich in spiritual truths, which I utilized for the betterment of my life.

In 2006 I started to use this particular knowledge to unveil the underlying meaning of the first ten chapters of Genesis in the Christian Bible. My interest in the Egyptian teachings sparked even more when I started deciphering the allegories, names, and symbolism contained within chapter 5 of the Genesis account. Knowing their meaning developed in me a higher sense of confidence that I had never felt before—like a knowing—which brought understanding and, finally, illumination in things of the spirit and about the world in general. As the present book owes a lot to Fabre d'Olivet's work, a few notes about him may be fitting.

Fabre d'Olivet was a writer during the time of the French Revolution. Born in 1769, d'Olivet belonged to a French Protestant family, descendants of the Camisards and Vaudois. Fred J. Mayers, author of *The Unknown God*, stated that d'Olivet studied Hebrew and Arabic under the tuition of German rabbis. He said that d'Olivet was already an excellent scholar of the classics, had an exceptionally wide knowledge of Greek and Latin literature, and later extended his studies to Sanskrit, Chinese, Samaritan, Syrian, Chaldee, and Ethiopian.

Mayers mentioned that d'Olivet's first important literary work collected from every possible source all the existing fragments of the "Golden Verses" of Pythagoras, which he translated and accompanied with a valuable philosophic commentary. This work was followed by *L'Histoire Philosophique du Genre Humain*, a large and important work that provided many writers with valuable material.

According to Mayers, d'Olivet's greatest achievement was *The Hebraic Tongue Restored*. Saint-Yves d'Alvedre, the author of *The Mission of the Jews*, described it as "the real monument, which will make the memory of Fabre d'Olivet immortal." He added, "Thanks to it the Sepher (The Book) is no longer a collection of tales of a grandmother, but a Book which is veritably sacred, and which contains the substance of all Truth and Science."

Fabre d'Olivet's interests were not theological but linguistic. He stated emphatically in his book that he had no intention whatsoever of making it a "commentary" on the Mosaic writings. "My sole purpose," d'Olivet said, "is to give my readers the means of reading and understanding those writings for themselves."[1]

Analyzing d'Olivet's greatest achievement (*The Hebraic Tongue Restored*) gave me the means to understand the underlying meaning of the first book of Moses. Chapter 5 of the Genesis account has been of great interest to me because it deals with the developing faculties of the universal mind and the beginning of man's creation.

Since my kabbalistic studies have taught me that the universal mind is formed of the assemblage of all minds (humanity), I was highly interested in discovering what constituted the faculties of the universal mind. I desired to know and understand them, thereby enabling me to develop them to achieve a higher level of consciousness and to help me in my progression toward ascension. I, in turn, desire to pass to the rest of humanity the same opportunity.

It is my intention not to profane any secrets learned through my association with mystical organizations. I desire that the mysteries I shall reveal as we go on will disturb no one. If, contrary to my expectation, some sectarians are found who might take offense at the publicity I give to certain mysteries, I say this to them: since I did not receive them from any person or society and have acquired them by my own studies alone, I can publish them without betraying any kind of oath.

SCRIPTURAL SYMBOLISM REVEALED

While the greatest minds of the Jewish and Christian worlds have realized that the Bible is a book of allegories, I learned that few seem to have taken the trouble to investigate its symbols and parables. Manly P. Hall, for example, author of *The Secret Teachings of All Ages,* stated that "there is no doubt that much of the material recorded in the first five books of the Old Testament is derived from the initiatory rituals of the Egyptian Mysteries. The Old Testament—especially the Pentateuch (the first five books of Moses)—contains not only the traditional account of the creation of the world and of man, but also locked within it are the secrets of the Egyptian initiators of the *Moses* concerning the genesis of god-man (the initiate) and the mystery of his rebirth (ascension from darkness) through philosophy" (pp. cxxxiii, cxxv). Such philosophy aims at an explanation of all the phenomena of the universe by ultimate causes.

In his book, *The Hebraic Tongue Restored*, Fabre d'Olivet claimed, "The Bible, which we possess, is far from being the exact translation of the Sepher (book) of Moses." He resorted to reestablishing the Hebrew tongue in its original principles. He accomplished this by throwing off the Hellenistic yoke (a mixture of Greek Hebraism); by reconstructing its lexicon (a dictionary or vocabulary of the Hebrew tongue); by penetrating the sanctuaries of the Essenes (regarded as among the better-educated class of Jews who enjoyed a merited reputation for learning and sanctity); and by opening at last that holy ark, which for more than three thousand years was closed to the profane and has brought down to us, by a decree of divine providence, the treasures amassed by the wisdom of the Egyptians.

The wisdom of the Egyptians, therefore, provides philosophical or kabbalistic keys (secret doctrines) by which allegories are made to reveal their hidden significance. The Jews called these philosophical keys to their sacred writings the *Kabbalah*, which comes from a Hebrew word that "literally signifies, that which is received, that which comes from elsewhere, that which is passed from hand to hand."[2] By using these keys, I removed the covers enveloping the knowledge underlying the scriptural symbolism in Genesis 5 and rendered it intelligible.

In successive steps, I offer a practical application of what was revealed, requiring the reader to form a hypothesis, come to a conclusion, or apply information in a new way. A summary is also offered as a concise review of the material given. Readers may read the summary before beginning the chapter to preview the topics, and they may also use them to refresh their memory after they have a firm grasp of the concepts presented in each chapter. Sections for critical thinking contain questions that test basic recall of the chapter's key points. Answers to these questions appear in Appendix B.

A PERSONAL NOTE

The study portrayed in this book is arranged to provoke and arouse divine impressions and revelations. By visualizing the material given— and after a few moments of concentration—one may discover that he has become attuned with some intelligence that assists in building up pictures consistent with what is being revealed in the chapters. This indicates that the individual is receiving an active form of manifestation from the universal mind. The reader will get the utmost out of these esoteric writings only if, on reading each chapter a second time, he or she takes one paragraph at a time and reads it slowly and carefully until the material has registered. Visualizing the written work and letting it build into lessons, beautiful pictures, and fascinating revelations will aid the reader in experiencing esoteric attunements that come from a carefully prepared kabbalistic rendering of Genesis 5.

SPECIAL NOTE TO ALL READERS

Throughout this book, I endeavored to clarify words and terms used to explain the verses. However, I am aware that some words may have escaped scrutiny. Therefore, I encourage the reader to employ the use of a dictionary if he comes across unfamiliar words or terms.

---

1. *The Unknown God* by F. J. Mayers.

2. *The Hebraic Tongue Restored* by Fabre d'Olivet.

1

GENERATIONS OF THE UNIVERSAL MIND

GENESIS 5:1

- Translation from the King James Version of the Bible: "This *is* the book of the generations of Adam in the day that God created man, in the likeness of God made he him."
- The literal English translation as it appears in *The Hebraic Tongue Restored*: "This is the book of the *symbolical-progenies* of *Adam*, at the day that creating, HE—the Gods, Adam (collective man) in the like-making-like HIM the Gods, he made the selfsameness—his."
- Transliteration from *The Hebraic Tongue Restored*: "Zeh Sepher Thô-ledôth Adam B'iôm beroà Ælohîm Adam bi-demoûth Ælohîm hashah âoth-ô."

All concepts, names, and numbers in Genesis 5 are a prelude to creation of physical mankind and must be regarded spiritually, not physically.

PROEM

From the verse given above, we will examine the words *generations* and *Adam*. Their examination is crucial to understanding the names

1

and numbers given in Genesis 5. Names and numbers were employed by Moses to:

- Connect stages of development in the Universal Mind;
- Express concepts;
- Describe abstract ideas, attributes or qualities, properties of the mind, and virtues; and
- Communicate universal mysteries and all the operations of the soul.

GENERATIONS

Various ways of writing and significations have been given to the word *generations*. For instance, James Strong, LLD, STD, author of *Strong's Exhaustive Concordance of the Bible*, and H. W. F. Gesenius, author of *Gesenius' Hebrew-Chaldee Lexicon to the Old Testament*, both show the Hebrew word for *generation* written as *towldah*, *toldah*, or *tholdoth* (Strong's/Gesenius' #8435), and as far as Genesis 5 is concerned, they say it means "descent, family, generations, races, and history." No other meanings are attached.

However, in the original Hebrew tongue, as reestablished and proved by the radical analysis in *The Hebraic Tongue Restored* (*THTR*), the Hebrew word for *generations* is actually composed of two words, *thô-ledôth* ("Cosmogony of Moses," *THTR*, 66, 150), which have distinctively different meanings. The radical vocabulary (a series of Hebrew roots) provided by *THTR* reveals that *tho* is a root containing every idea of a sign, symbol, or hieroglyphic character. It is taken, in a restricted sense, for the same thing symbolized and for that which serves to symbolize. It is, then, a narration, a fable, a speech, a table, a book. It is a description, a monument, an emblem, etc.

2

Universal Mind Revealed

The word *ledôth* is the image of every emanation and expresses every idea of propagation or generation or any extension whatsoever given to being: that which is born, generated, propagated, or bred— or progeny, increase of family, race, lineage, confinement, childbirth, etc. Therefore, the above description of *thô-ledôth*, in conveying the word *generations*, is actually used as a symbol of something else and denotes that there is more than one meaning to the words that follow.

Thus Genesis 5:1 above should read: "This *is* the book of the symbolically described generations (progenies) of Adam" rather than "This *is* the book of the generations of Adam."

ADAM

The word that follows *generations* is *Adam*, denoting that *Adam* is symbolic of something else. Great majorities of people think that Adam was a human being or the first man. Others believe that *Adam* means "the human race." A few, realizing that the Bible is a book of allegories, spend time investigating a deeper meaning. These few employ reason and are able to discern what is said allegorically, figuratively, and hyperbolically[1] apart from what is meant literally.

The Egyptian priests, authors of this mysterious name and of a great part of those employed by Moses, presented the name Adam with three meanings—literal, figurative, and hieroglyphical. This conforms to the Essenian[2] tradition, which says that every word in the book of Moses in the Christian Bible contains three meanings: the simple or literal (easily understood as presented), the figurative (metaphorical), and the hieratic (surpassing all other interpretations). We will proceed to investigate the three meanings given to the name *Adam*: literally as the "kingdom of mind," figuratively as the "resemblance of Ælohîm,"[3] and hieroglyphically as the "one becoming the many."

3

LITERAL MEANING OF THE NAME *ADAM*

The name *Adam* signifies not only *homo* man, but—as the Samaritan version of the Bible clearly saw in rendering *Adam* as "universal" (better understood as "mankind")—Adam is better expressed as "Kingdom of Man" ("Cosmogony of Moses," *THTR*, 58).

The Hebrew scholar, philologist, and initiate Fabre d'Olivet (FD'O), author of *The Hebraic Tongue Restored*, states that the literal meaning of the name *Adam* is "Kingdom of Man; it is Collective Man, Man abstractly formed of the assemblage of all men" (ibid.). His translation of this Hebrew noun proves accurate when the components of the name *Adam*—"Ad" and "m"—are studied individually.

The root "Ad" with the collective sign "m" at the end denotes uniting by abstraction into one single being (the so-called first man) all those of the same kind (*THTR*, 385).

In "Adam," all *beings* resembling him are united by abstraction. The word *abstraction* means that the kingdom of man is separately and absolutely, in state or manner, unconnected and unlinked to any other kingdom in nature, such as the mineral, plant, or animal kingdoms.

We do not need to think very hard to see that Adam is not a human, for in what single human being could all those of the same kind be united by abstraction? Or what single human being (man) can be universal? The answer is found in the meaning of the words *man* and *mind*.

MEANING OF *MAN* AND *MIND*

Webster's Unabridged Dictionary (1946) states that the word *man* comes from the Sanskrit[4] word *manu*, and *manu* comes from the root word *man*, meaning: "to think." According to Webster, to "think"

4

is to utilize one's mind, to bring the intellectual faculties into play. These are the understanding or intellectual capacities of the mind.

Webster says that *mind* is a synonym for *soul*. Webster also states that the word *mind* in Anglo Saxon is *gemynd*, which means "memory, thought," or *munan*, "to think," or *gemunan*, "to remember." It is akin to the Icelandic *minni*, Gothic *gamunds*, Latin *mens*, Greek *menos*, and Sanskrit *manas*, which mean: "mind, man, to think." Therefore, the words *man* and *mind* are synonymous, as are the words *mind* and *soul*. That is to say, when we talk about the "kingdom of man," we are also referring to the kingdom of mind or soul, for they are one and the same.

With the information thus garnered above, it can now be safely deduced that:

1. Adam is the "kingdom of mind."
2. Adam is "collective mind," mind that is abstractly, absolutely, and separately unconnected and not linked to any other kingdom of nature.
3. As the collective mind, Adam is formed of the assemblage of all minds. It unites by abstraction or separates in one single being (Adam) all those of the same kind. Therefore, Adam is "universal mind" or "universal soul" containing all those of the same kind—that is, containing all minds or souls resembling Adam's. This knowledge tells us that "Adam" is to be a "group soul," a living creature for all souls or minds.
4. The name *Adam* denotes a kingdom, and it is the name of what humanity has come to recognize as the kingdom of man.

FIGURATIVE MEANING OF THE NAME *ADAM*

Figuratively, the noun *Adam* denotes assimilation, likeness, or pictorial representation of something else ("Cosmogony of Moses," *THTR*, 58).

Etymologically, the word *Adam* means "potential likeness" or "potential assimilation." *Assimilation* is "the act of bringing to a resemblance." It is the process by which bodies convert other bodies into their own nature and substance (as flame assimilates oil) or into their own qualities or appearance (Webster, 1946).

Assimilation refers to the similitude or likeness of substance, the homogeneity, the character or quality of being homogeneous. The word *homogeneous* is derived from the Greek words *homos*, which means: "the same," and *genos*, which means "race, family, kind" (Webster, 1946). Adam, therefore, is of the same character—essentially like and of the same or nearly the same nature—as his maker.

This signifies that Adam was brought to a resemblance of Ælohîm, his maker. "And God said, 'Let us make man[5] in our image, after our likeness'" (Genesis 1:26). Simply put, it was in the image of the manifold attributes of Ælohîm that Adam was made. That is to say, Adam is the microcosm of Ælohîm, the epitome of Ælohîm in a condensed form. Therefore, Adam is endowed with the assimilative qualities of Ælohîm, making him the perfect prototype (original model) and source of all the souls of humanity, whereby the one (Adam) becomes the many (humanity) in the new cycle of evolution.

Moreover, the Hebrew root "dm" (radical vocabulary, THTR, 323)—part of the name *Adam*—being governed by the sign of power and stability, "A" (ibid., 287), becomes the image of an immortal assimilation (of resemblance, nature, and substance), and of an aggregation of homogeneous and indestructible parts. Thus Adam,

6

or "universal mind," is immortal, meaning "not mortal," exempt from liability to death, having unlimited existence, undying, an immortal soul that is incapable of being destroyed. This is contrary to the teaching of the church, which founded its doctrine of salvation upon the so-called death of Adam.

HIEROGLYPHIC MEANING OF THE NAME *ADAM*

To find the hieroglyphic meaning of Adam, we must resort to interpreting each Hebrew sign composing the name Adam: "A," "D," and "M."

The Hebrew Signs: "A" and "D"

The radical vocabulary (p. 287) explains the Hebrew sign "A" is the principiant power. It coincides with the meaning of the symbolic number one in the general signification of the Hebraic decade ("Cosmogony of Moses," THTR, 306). That is, number one indicates "principiation" (beginning) and "stability" (refer to "Symbolic Writings" in Appendix A). That is to say, all appears in power of being first—not yet in action but in germ (the principle from which anything proceeds). It is primordial substance, the vital source or necessary first cause that gives rise to principiation. Therefore, the Hebrew sign "A" in the name *Adam* is the beginning, the central point unfolding the circumference (the material world, or established limit of a selected creative area).

The Hebrew sign "D" denotes multiplication and divisional abundance (radical vocabulary, THTR, 318) and coincides with the meaning of the symbolic number four in the general signification of the Hebraic decade. That is, number four indicates divisional multiplication: the whole (the germ) is divided into parts; it is abundance born of division. "D" is the sign of physical divisibility and divided nature. It signifies things becoming numerous by subdivision. Therefore, the natural constitution or quality of Adam (universal mind) is to form into divisions, to classify, or to arrange— as a genus into species. Adam becomes numerous by subdivision.

The signs "A" and "D," united, disclose the "one becoming the many," the Adam becoming the assemblage of all minds (humanity). It indicates that the number one has been divided and multiplied as a result of division.

The Hebrew Root, "AD," and the Hebrew Sign, "M"

The Hebrew root "AD," when endowed with the collective sign "M" at the end of the name *Adam* (AD-M), becomes the collective sign, developing Adam in infinite space as far as his divisible and divided nature permits (radical vocabulary, THTR, 385) within his predetermined area of activity or material center (the circumference). Adam (universal mind) assumes an unlimited development within this center because of the collective sign "M." That is to say, when the symbolic number ten is taken to represent the Hebrew root "AD" (the one becoming the many), the sign "M" will develop its progressive power as one hundred, one thousand, and ten thousand ... to infinity.

Further, the collective sign "M" unites by abstraction into one single being (Adam) all those of the same kind, all those that are made in Adam's likeness: mankind. Therefore, mankind makes up the sum total of all minds.

We can now determine, by the above significations of the name *Adam* and the word *generations*, that the story of Genesis 5:1 relates to the existence of a book of symbolically described progenies of the universal mind (Adam). Further along in this book, we shall see that the progenies of Adam are his developing mental faculties and his thought states that proceeded successively when Adam came forth in its perfection as the image of Ælohîm. We will learn that the symbolic progenies are the conception, origin, and source of the beginning of all ideas of fructification, production, and elementary generation of Adam's faculties (the so-called "patriarchs" of Genesis). Finally, Genesis 5:1 relates to us the commencement or entrance into being.

SUMMARY

The word *generations*, as portrayed in Genesis 5:1, is used as a symbol of something else, denoting that there is more than one meaning to the words that follow. Thus Genesis 5:1 above should read: "This *is* the book of the symbolically described generations (progenies) of Adam" rather than "This *is* the book of the generations of Adam."

The name *Adam* follows the word *generations*; therefore it is symbolic of something else. Egyptian wisdom renders this name in three different ways: literal, figurative, and hieroglyphical. The literal meaning renders *Adam* as the "universal mind. Figuratively, it is the "resemblance of Ælohîm." Hieroglyphically, it is the "one becoming the many."

As the universal mind, Adam contains within himself all minds resembling his. This knowledge tells us that Adam is a "group soul," a "living creature" for all minds. The name *Adam*, then, denotes a kingdom and is the name of what humanity has come to recognize as the kingdom of man.

As a resemblance of Ælohîm, Adam was made in the image of the manifold attributes of Ælohîm. He is the microcosm of Ælohîm, the epitome of Ælohîm in a condensed form, and therefore he is endowed with the assimilative qualities of Ælohîm, making him the perfect prototype (original model) and source of all the souls of humanity whereby the one (Adam) becomes the many (humanity) in the new cycle of evolution.

As the one becoming the many, Adam's natural constitution or quality is to form into divisions, to classify, or to arrange—as a genus into species. He becomes numerous by subdivision.

★ *PRACTICAL APPLICATION*

In this chapter, we learned that the universal mind is formed of the assemblage of all minds and that humanity composes this assemblage. We must realize that since there is but one mind in the entire universe, its essence and intelligence function through the physical bodies of all human beings; and since our physical body is of the earth (which is transitory), we must not become conscious of it but of the mind in it (which is immortal). That mind—being the one mind, the only mind, and our consciousness being of and in that mind—constitutes a unit of the universal mind.

As a unit of the universal mind, we can come in contact with it by extending our consciousness into the broad universal consciousness of this great mind. We can lift our soul, the spiritual part of ourselves, to attune with all the wisdom this universal mind has, for "the heart of the prudent gets knowledge; and the ear of the wise seeks knowledge" (Proverbs 18:15). During the time of our contact, we can think, not as individuals or earthly personalities, but as a universal mind, a universal being building ourselves with wisdom so that understanding can be established.

CRITICAL THINKING

1. In the Hebraic text, the word *generations* is used as a symbol to denote that there is more than one meaning to the words that follow. *Adam* follows this word. How many meanings are attributed to the name *Adam*? Name them.

2. Adam has been rendered as "universal" and is better expressed as the "kingdom of man" or the "collective man," which is abstractly formed by the assemblage of all men. What does the word *abstractly* connote when referring to the kingdom of man?

3. According to *Webster's Unabridged Dictionary* (1946), the words *man, mind*, and *soul* are synonymous. *Adam* is therefore "universal mind" or "universal soul." What does this knowledge tell us?

4. The assimilative qualities of the Adam (universal mind) enable him to convert other bodies into his own nature and substance, or into his own qualities or appearance. Explain.

5. The universal mind (Adam) is immortal. Why is this so?

6. The universal mind's natural constitution or quality is to form into divisions, to classify, or to arrange—as a genus into species. Explain.

7. The universal mind assumes an unlimited development within its center of activity. Is man's mind endowed with this same capability? If yes, why? If not, why not?

8. What develops within the mind?

(Answers in Appendix B)

1.   *Hyperbolical* refers to a statement of anything as being much greater or less than the reality.

2.   Essenians were regarded as among the better-educated class of Jews. They were most prominent in the early Syrian sects. Some authorities trace them back to the schools of Samuel, the prophet, but most agree on either an Egyptian or Oriental origin (*The Secret Teachings of All Ages*).

3.   *Ælohîm* is the plural of the word *Æloah*, the name given to the Supreme Being by the Hebrews and the Chaldeans. It is derived from the root "AL" and depicts elevation, strength, and expansive power, signifying in a universal sense, God. *Ælohîm* signifies exactly this: "HE-They-who-are: the Being of beings" (FD'O, 28). The Kabbalist F. J. Mayers renders *Ælohîm* as, "HE, the unity of Gods."

4.   Webster's dictionary describes *Sanskrit* as the ancient language of the Hindus, in which most of their vast literature is written, from the oldest portion of the Vedas (the sacred Sanskrit writings of the ancient Hindus supposed to date from about 1500 BC) downward, though it has long ceased to be a living and spoken language. It is one of the Aryan or Indo-European families of tongues and may be described as an elder sister of the Persian, Greek, Latin, Teutonic, Slavonic, and Celtic tongues. To the modern Aryan languages of India, it stands in the same relation as Latin stands to the Romance languages. It is a highly inflected language, having in this respect many resemblances to Greek.

To philologists it has proved, perhaps, the most valuable of tongues. It was only after it became known to Europeans that philology began to assume the character of a science. Its supreme value is due to the transparency of its structure and to its freedom from the corrupting and disguising effect of phonetic change and from obliteration of the original meaning of its vocables.

Fabre d'Olivet differs from Webster's dictionary in that he says that Sanskrit did not have its origin in India. He believes that a people much older than the Hindus, people who inhabited another region of the earth, came in very remote times to be established in Bharat-Wersh, today's Hindustan, and brought there a celebrated idiom called Bali or Pali, many indications of which are found in Singhala of the island of Ceylon, in the kingdoms of Siam and Pegu, and in all of what was called the empire of the Burmans (*The Hebraic Tongue Restored*, 14).

5.   *Man*: The transliterated Hebrew words in Genesis 1:26 state that Ælohîm said, "We will make 'Adam' (universal man) in our reflected Shadow (image) after the laws of our assimilating action" (*The Hebraic Tongue Restored*, 311–312). The current interpretation given in the Christian Bible is a mistranslation.

2

UNIVERSALITY OF THE MALE AND FEMALE PRINCIPLE

GENESIS 5:2

- Translation from the King James Version of the Bible: "Male and female created he them and blessed them, and called their name Adam, in the day when they were created."
- The literal English translation as it appears in *The Hebraic Tongue Restored*: "Male and female, he created them and he blessed them, and he assigned this universal name Adam, at the day of the being created them universally."
- Transliteration from *The Hebraic Tongue Restored*: "Zacher w-nekebah bherâ am wa-îbarech âoth am, wa-îkerâ æth-shemam Adam b'iôm bi-barâm."

Except for the proem in this chapter, the following interpretation of Genesis 5:2 is spiritual in nature, not physical.

PROEM

One unique truth about man's powers is his ability to copulate or unite in sexual union, to procreate or to generate and produce other beings for the advancement of the human species. We can also see in all creation the fecundity (or power of germinating), which perpetuates and rejuvenates the world's existence. We can witness that in fecundity the male and female principles are always contributory. This contribution is commonly viewed as the sex principle in divine manifestation. They are viewed as two essences, one (the male ♂) being dynamic, replete, and fecundating, and the other (the female ♀) being static, receptive, and reproductive.

MALE AND FEMALE PRINCIPLES OF THE UNIVERSAL MIND

The Kabbalah reveals that the male/female principle also exists in the universal mind (Adam). Genesis 5:2 above validates this existence and conveys that the male/female aspects of Adam were created "universally." Further, it conveys that the name *Adam* is a "universal" name. *Adam*, being a universal name, could not know a companion, for the Hebraic word *Adam* has no feminine. Adam, however, was endowed (blessed) with this dual faculty, which the Kabbalah designates as "Aish" and "Aishah" respectively: the male and female principles. The wisdom of the Egyptians reveals this dual faculty was a new development of the universal mind.

In the universal mind, the male and female principles are rendered as "intellect" (♂) and "will" (♀) ("Cosmogony of Moses," THTR, 89–91). The intellect serves as an instrument to receive or comprehend ideas communicated by the senses or by perception. Intelligence enables the universal mind to know or understand, while the will (the female principle) serves as its principiant volitive faculty (ibid., 90).[1]

As a principiant volitive faculty, the female principle gives the universal mind an independent individuality (separate or distinct existence) and leaves the universal mind free to manifest itself in other and particular conceptions by means of its auxiliary force (the female principle) intended to reflect its image (ibid., 91, 93).

As a principiant volitive faculty, the female principle impels (or incites) the universal mind to act on its conceptions. This volitive faculty is the dynamo that feeds all powers or faculties of the universal mind. It initiates and keeps in continuous operation all activities of the universal mind.

The female principle was created by the "Being of beings" (ibid., 92) from the latent faculty of "intellect" (ibid., 91), and this latent faculty was that part of the universal mind called "apprehension" or "comprehension." By this, the female principle of the universal mind enables it to conceive and understand new ideas through the intellect. Thus, bestowed within the universal mind is the divine female faculty that is identifiable with the divine faculties of intelligence and with the creative power of God's Word and Will. The Word and Will are then reflected in the universal mind so that it can manifest what God created in principle.

DUAL POLARITIES OF THE UNIVERSAL MIND

The male and female principles are conceived as dual polarities within the universal mind, the male element being positive and the female being negative, like the positive and negative polarities of electrical charges that underlie all electrical phenomena. Their attraction and union keep the universal mind active and in motion. They are the forces of creation, the relation of contraries in nature, and the polarities upon which all creation and manifestation depend.

In other words, the male/female or sex principle represents the dual (or united male/female) aspects of creation, which is always visible in evolution: in spirit (♂) and matter (♀); life (♂) and form (♀); fire (♂) and water (♀); air (♂) and earth (♀); love (♂) and wisdom (♀); mind (♂) and emotion (♀); intellect (♂) and intuition (♀).

Everything existing, says the Zohar[2], can only be the work of the male and female principles—understandably so, since, according to Genesis 5:2, they were made universal[3] and have the capacity to be *in* everything.

Hidden Wisdom in the Holy Bible (Vol. 1, 155–156) explains the male/female aspect of creation in this manner: Spirit is the masculine creative potency, the male participant in all generative processes. Substance, the matter of space and the feminine creative potency, is the female participant in all generative processes.

The feminine aspect of creation suggests both the infinite reproductiveness of matter and the fertility of nature, which perpetually provides abundance and is therefore regarded as a prolific image.

The Hebrew text describes the male/female principle as follows: the male principle or "Zacher" is the cause, or "that which impels into existence." It is the reason or motive that urges and moves the mind to make decisions. It moves and gives direction to existence and is conformable to a given model resembling that, which is conceived, generated, and increased. It is the commencement or entrance into existence.

The female principle, or "Nekebah," is the means used to attain an end. That is, it is used to bring forth the conceptions of the mind. It is the medium through which anything is done or carried out, a measure employed to effect a purpose, an agency, or an instrumentality. It is an extraordinary movement of material existence that gives form to unformed matter.

MALE/FEMALE PRINCIPLE AT WORK

A good example of this dual principle at work is the life cycle of advanced multicellular animals, including humans. The male sex organ produces sperm, and the female sex organ produces eggs. A new individual comes into existence when the sperm (or seed) of the male fertilizes the egg of the female. The male sperm (the cause) impels into existence when it enters the egg (the means). The egg is the ground for the seed to take root, grow, and form amorphous matter (the sperm and the egg) into a solid individual (formed matter).

Figure 2.1 below depicts the endowment of the male/ female principle to the universal mind.

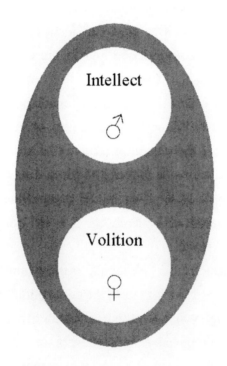

ADAM'S MICROCOSM (1/10)

Like Ælohîm, Adam possesses a microcosm. His microcosm is like a tent in which his intellect and volitive faculties dwell together in the mind, but as depicted in Figure 2.1, the faculties still keep their own embodiment (individuality). The Kabbalah reveals that the "Being of beings" endowed these two faculties to Adam (universal mind). These endowments enable Adam to develop his other faculties, and these individual attributes will be included in this tent as he evolves in infinite space (as far as his nature permits) within his predetermined material center.

SUMMARY

Genesis 5:2 reveals that the male and female principles are always contributory in the fecundity of creation. Their contribution is viewed as two essences, one (the male) being dynamic, replete, and fecundating, and the other (the female) being static, receptive, and reproductive.

This dual principle also exists in the universal mind, and the two aspects are rendered as intellect (male) and will (female). The intellect receives or comprehends ideas communicated by the senses or by perception, while the will impels the mind to act in its conceptions.

The female principle is the volitive faculty of the mind. It initiates and keeps in continuous operation all activities of the mind.

The male/female principle is conceived as dual polarities (positive and negative) within the universal mind. They are the forces of creation and the contraries in nature.

The male principle impels things into existence, while the female is the means to attain that end.

★ *PRACTICAL APPLICATION*

In this chapter we learned that the male and female principles are conceived as dual polarities of the universal mind. In the universal mind, this dual faculty is rendered as intellect (male) and will or volition (female). Further, we learned in chapter 1 that humanity is an extension of this great mind. As such, the male and female principles of the universal mind are inborn in man.

How can the universality of these innate principles be of use to us? Possessing this dual faculty enables us to create concepts in our minds (male aspect) and to utilize our will or volition (female aspect) to actualize such conceptions. We become aware that by exercising our volitive faculty we do not get discouraged after one—or perhaps several—unsuccessful efforts. Instead we continue with unceasing determination and action revolving around the desires of our mind, until our volitive faculty becomes dynamic enough to produce the much-craved result. With volition, we will and act until victory. No matter how impossible the accomplishment of our goal may seem, with volition we will keep repeating conscious acts to achieve our goal for as long as we live.

CRITICAL THINKING

1. Man copulates in sexual union to generate and produce other beings for the advancement of the human species. Is copulation an ability that only man possesses?
2. The male/female principle is a dual faculty of the mind. How is this dual principle rendered in the universal mind?
3. The female principle is an auxiliary force of the mind. Describe its purpose.
4. Intellect and will are faculties of the mind. Describe how they function.
5. Of the two faculties described in this chapter, which one individualized the mind?
6. The female principle is the volitive faculty of the mind. As a volitive faculty, what are its functions?

7. The male and female principles are conceived as dual polarities within the universal mind; one is negative and the other is positive. Since we learned in chapter 1 that humanity is part of the universal mind, are these polarities also within the mind of man?

8. How do these positive and negative polarities interact within the human mind and all creation?

9. Which one of the two principles is in activity when making a decision?

10. Which medium is employed to bring forth the mind's conceptions?

(Answers in Appendix B)

[1.] *Principiant volitive faculty* is not the volitive principle, which exists only in power; it is the principiant *will* that exists no longer in power but in action (THTR, 92–93).

[2.] *Zohar* is a Jewish book of kabbalistic commentaries on Scriptures.

[3.] Webster's dictionary describes the word *universal* as "that, which by its nature is fit to be predicated of many, which by its nature has a fitness or capacity to be in many." This description of the word *universal* fits the hieroglyphic interpretation given to the Hebrew signs "A" and "D" in the name Adam, "A" signifying "one" and "D" signifying "becoming the many" or "the one becoming the many." (Refer to the hieroglyphic meaning of the name *Adam* in chapter 1.)

3

FOUNDATION OF THE SOUL: SHETH

GENESIS 5:3

- Translation from the King James Version of the Bible: "And Adam lived an hundred and thirty years and begat a son in his own likeness, after his image; and called his name Seth."
- The literal English translation as it appears in *The Hebraic Tongue Restored*: "And he was being, Adam, three-tens and one-hundred (extension, stretching), of being's temporal revolving change; and he begat by the like making like himself, in the shadow-his-own (an issued offspring) and he assigned this name to him, Sheth."
- Transliteration from *The Hebraic Tongue Restored*: "Wa-îhî Adam sheloshîm w-mâth shanah, wa-iôled bi-demouth-ô b'tzalem-ô wa-îkerâ aeth-shem-ô Sheth."

The following interpretation of Genesis 5:3 is spiritual in nature, not physical.

PROEM

Just as houses must first have their foundations before their frames and walls are built, so the souls of men must first have their foundations or substratums to support their mental, emotional, astral, and physical vestments—these being the vehicles of consciousness in which souls function. Genesis 5:3 relates how the universal mind began the process of building up the souls' foundations by first developing its own faculty or power that would enable it to create the foundations. This can be likened to creating a blueprint of a house and then building houses following the precepts set forth in the blueprint.

Genesis 5:3 further conveys that the universal mind (Adam) named this new faculty *Sheth.* Assigning a name personified the faculty and discloses the procedure and stage of development in the unfolding universal mind. The Hebrew text reveals that Sheth's distinguishing qualities gave the universal mind the power to frame the foundations or substrata for the perceptible qualities of the souls to inhere or adhere to. This knowledge will be elaborated upon in chapters 7 and 8.

The steps taken to develop the new faculty are hidden under the allegory (metaphor) and symbology of the Hebrew words and the number one hundred and thirty given above. The first Hebrew word presented for consideration is *îhî*. *Îhî* relates to us the manifestation of elementary existence, which renders being manifest and obvious.

ELEMENTARY EXISTENCE

The Hebrew word *îhî* denotes the following:

- The manifestation of elementary existence: the rudimentary, primary, initial, and simple vital aspiration (inhaling life) that renders being manifest and obvious
- The kind of life that seeks an outlet or some means of expressing itself
- The kind of life that demands effort, care, and fatigue
- Life that strains to accomplish through labor. This can be better understood as the formative activities or impulses of the

universal mind upon elementary existence to render elements (electrons, protons, and other constituent ingredients) manifest and obvious, which subsequently enables the universal mind to build its faculties and their similitudes

The number 130 elaborates on the steps taken to produce the faculty that will give the universal mind the power to frame the substrata[1] of the immortal souls.

UNDERLYING MEANING OF THE NUMBER 130

We will begin our interpretation of the number 130 by analyzing the two names composing this number: *Sheloshîm* (number thirty) and *Mâth* (number one hundred). Consideration will also be given to the name *Shelosh*, the radical number three, because thirty is a decuple number of three. Decuple numbers are numbers that are tenfold of their radical number—as ten is to one, twenty is to two, thirty is to three, forty is to four, fifty is to five, sixty is to six, seventy is to seven, eighty is to eight, and ninety is to nine.

All decuple numbers are formed from the plural of their primitive or radical number—that is, the radical number is repeated or multiplied ten times. A decuple number is only the complement of its radical number. Therefore, in this verse consideration will also be given to the latter in order to extract the concise meaning underlying number thirty.

The number one hundred, considered a centuple, is the most simple of arithmetic forms. It is a collection, body, or sum consisting of ten times ten individuals or units. In more complex mathematical computations, one hundred has infinite decuple powers, i.e., one hundred, one thousand, ten thousand, etc. In the Hebrew tongue, the name of this number, *Mâth* or *Mœôth*, indicates an extension produced by a desire to extend or manifest something exteriorly. Let us now proceed with an examination of the numbers thirty and one hundred.

Number Thirty: *Sheloshîm*

To extract the meaning of *sheloshîm* we must separate this word into its simplest components—*sh-she-el-shl-l-lo-losh-lsh-osh-shi-im*—and then obtain their meaning from the radical vocabulary.

The Hebrew text presents three parts to the understanding of these simple components: the noun, the verb, and the relation (a logical or natural association between the noun and the verb). After a comprehensive analysis of these three parts, *sheloshîm* reveals this: The universal mind (Adam) descended into its sphere of activity[2] to extend, rise, and unfold the elements extracted from elementary existence.

Descension into the sphere of activity was an eccentric movement that stretched in all directions (east, west, north, south, northeast, northwest, southeast, southwest, and depth) to carry the elements forward.

This eccentric movement expanded the intellectual powers of the universal mind. It enabled it to understand how to progressively build its new faculty. That is to say, the universal mind understood how to unite the elements into atoms, and subsequently, how to create coalitions that would unite the atoms into a mass.

Coalitions led the universal mind to concatenate or link atoms together in successive series; that is, the atoms were kept fixed in union with a degree of density or spissitude, not perfectly liquid, not perfectly solid, but indefinite and depending on each other to form liaisons or create bonds that maintained their union.

In his book, *Conceptual Physics* (p. 185), Paul G. Hewitt explains this phenomenon. He states, "When atoms are close together, the negative electrons of one atom may at times be closer to the positive nucleus of another atom, which results in a net attraction between the atoms. That is why some atoms combine to form molecules" or denser mass. It is likened to making the atoms stick together by natural attraction, as the atoms of homogeneous bodies unite in a mass, or as the force, which makes the parts of matter move toward each other, brings them to aggregation, accumulation, and union, thus bonding universally.

The motion of natural forces unfolding and acting within the universal mind was an expanding movement conceived abstractly as a line going from one point to another—softening, kneading, and making the firm, unyielding, and divided formless matter ductile. In other words, matter was being influenced. It yielded to instructions from the universal mind. This enabled the universal mind to unite *en masse*—to form, compose, shape, fashion, adjust, settle, put together, and arrange the different qualities of its evolving faculty and its various aspects within matter. Consequently, a real and evident existence became obvious.

Following the above kabbalistic interpretation of number thirty, let us now consider its primitive or radical number three.

Number Three: *Shelosh*

Number three sums up the activities mentioned in number thirty. By the number three we understand every extraction (drawing out) or subtraction (operating or taking a part from the whole), every amalgamation, every kneading together. That is to say, developing the new faculty entailed (1) a *movement* of extraction by taking elements or constituent parts from elementary existence (the primordial substance) and (2) *amalgamating* the separate elements by kneading them together into a well-mixed mass, which resulted in (3) the *creation* of a new existence, a homogeneous body united into a mass.

Number One Hundred: *Mâth*

Number one hundred, or *mâth*, reveals an extension was produced by the desire of the universal mind to extend and manifest its conception. Thence, the number one hundred in this verse conveys the new existence (referred to above) developed to the extent the universal mind desired it to extend, dilate, and manifest exteriorly, which was to the extent the universal mind had developed.

MICROCOSM OF THE UNIVERSAL MIND

The Hebrew words *bi-demouth-ô b'tzalem-ô wa-îkerâ aeth-shem-ô Sheth* given in the transliterated version of Genesis 5:3 reveal the following:

- The new faculty was made to resemble the universal mind (Adam) in form and qualities.
- The name *Sheth* was assigned to this new faculty. The Hebrew text states that the reason this faculty was named *Sheth* was because of its distinguishing qualities. That is to say, the distinguishing qualities or character of faculties are the reason why they get a particular name. It is not just a matter of calling anything by an arbitrary name.
- *Sheth* is the microcosm of the universal mind, its epitome in a condensed form.
- *Sheth* was passed from one state to another, evolving in the reflected shadow of the universal mind.

SHETH'S DISTINGUISHING QUALITIES

Sheth is that faculty that gives the universal mind the power to frame the foundation of the immortal soul. This foundation establishes a solid ground on which the perceptible qualities (mental, emotional, astral, and physical vestures) of the soul inhere. It is the basis, the groundwork of the soul—its underlying principle. And since Genesis 5:3 makes known that this faculty was made in the likeness of its maker, the universal mind, then Sheth's distinguishing qualities encompass the intellect, knowledge, and consciousness of all the Truth inherited from the consciousness of Ælohîm, which the universal mind possesses. (Refer to the figurative meaning of the name *Adam* in chapter 1.)

SHETH SUPPORTING THE PERCEPTIBLE QUALITIES OF THE SOUL

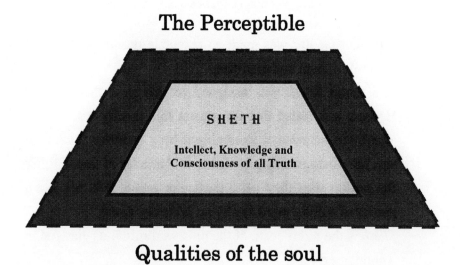

Figure 3.1. The perceptible qualities of the soul are shown here in broken lines to indicate their temporary nature. *Sheth* is shown in solid lines to indicate its permanence.

ADAM'S MICROCOSM (2/10)

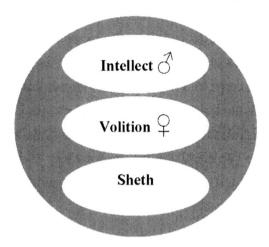

Figure 3.2 above shows the growing faculties of Adam are now composed of intellect (male principle), volition/will (female principle), and *Sheth* (Adam's power to frame the foundation of the soul). Within the nature of Adam's microcosm, the Ælohîm establish all the qualities and powers that they themselves possess.

SUMMARY

Genesis 5:3 reveals the steps taken to develop the faculty that will enable the universal mind to build the foundation of the souls. It is the beginning stages of building a solid ground upon which the souls' vestments (mental, emotional, astral, and physical vehicles of the souls) will adhere to.

★ *PRACTICAL APPLICATION*

The underlying principle, the foundation of our soul, enables us to gather within it the efforts of our soul personality while transiting the physical world. Ancient teachings reveal that this underlying principle (Sheth) is the seat of our Higher Mind, and that through the Higher Mind we obtain wisdom, vigor, and life everlasting. As such, we must earnestly acquire knowledge and seek experiences that teach us the highest principle of spiritual living to enable us to unfold and gradually emerge into objective activity our latent qualities and faculties, which are housed within our Higher Mind. Because inner development is directed by conscious, continually experienced intelligence, we can eliminate the rudimentary and imperfect and can progress through the efforts of our soul personality or that which constitutes our character.

CRITICAL THINKING

1. The soul clothes itself with vestments. They are the mental, emotional, astral, and physical vestments. What is the soul's underlying principle in which these vestments inhere?
2. The steps taken to develop the underlying principle of the soul are hidden under scriptural allegories and symbols. What symbols are predominantly used by Moses to convey the making of this principle and of other faculties?
3. What is the knowledge conveyed under the number 130?
4. The universal mind created a faculty that will enable it to frame the foundation of the immortal soul. What is the name of this faculty?
5. Why was the name *Sheth* assigned to this faculty?
6. What are the distinguishing qualities of *Sheth*?
7. What are the perceptible qualities of the soul?

(Answers in Appendix B)

---

[1] Substrata is the matter or substance that furnishes the basis in which the perceptible qualities of the soul inhere.

[2] *Sphere of activity* is the circumference, the established limit of the selected creative area.

4

THE SOULS OF MEN: SIMILITUDES OF THE UNIVERSAL MIND, PART 1

GENESIS 5:4

- Translation from the King James Version of the Bible: "And the days of Adam after he had begotten Seth were eight hundred years and he begat sons and daughters."
- The literal English translation as it appears in *The Hebraic Tongue Restored*: "And they were the days (the manifested lights) of Adam, after the causing him to beget the selfsameness of Sheth, eight hundreds of revolving change: and he teemed sons and daughters (many issued beings)."
- Transliteration from *The Hebraic Tongue Restored*: "Wa-îhîou îmeî-Adam âhareî, hôlid-ô æth-Sheth shemoneh mâoth shanah wa-iôled banîm w'banôth."

The following interpretation of Genesis 5:4 is spiritual in nature, not physical.

PROEM

We learned in the previous chapter that the faculty that will enable the universal mind to build the foundations (groundwork) of the souls was generated and that these foundations are to be established for the qualities of the souls of men to inhere. Now, the generation of souls (symbolically known as the sons and daughters of Adam) follows. This is necessary for the evolution of consciousness, for it will make man a conscious being, possessing the power of knowing his own thoughts or mental operations.

Genesis 5:4 reveals that generating the souls was an intrinsic process involving the energetic, forceful, qualitative, and formative powers of the universal mind. The Hebrew words *îhîou îmeî âhareî* and *hôlid* reveal the preceding steps that led to the generation of the souls.

Îhîou reveals that the souls were arranged, prepared, and given agreeable forms during their luminous period of manifestation. *Îmeî* conveys that it involved mobilizing the spiritual creative waters[1] (where the elements of everything that is to exist are held in solution) to render elements manifest and obvious. That is, it required the universal mind to mobilize elementary existence to manifest constituent parts necessary to build the souls. *Âhareî* adds that the universal mind compressed and confined the elements from free movement in order to give them a definite form or expression that was compacted and centralized. This gave the souls their power of being, which, though not yet existing, were nevertheless found to have the power to exist.

Hôlid conveys that the universal mind bound their non-being to being by passing the centralized elements from one nature to another in an eccentric movement designed to extend, rise, and unfold the elements in all directions within its predetermined area of activity. Hence, the souls began to be knitted and cemented; they began to be framed, raised, or shaped into particular forms that resembled the universal mind in structure. That is, their homogeneous substance was formed by the affinity of similar constituent parts that held the same universal organization as that of Adam, the prototype of humanity.[2] Therefore, the souls circumscribed the extent of the universal mind (Adam).

The number eight hundred given in this verse reveals the intricacies of steps taken by the universal mind to develop the souls in its image.

UNDERLYING MEANING OF THE NUMBER 800

We will begin the interpretation of the number eight hundred by examining its two components: *shemoneh* (number eight) and *mâoth* (number one hundred).

Shemoneh signifies the action of placing, of putting one thing upon another, of specifying or designating things by name so as to distinguish one thing from another. It is the action of distinguishing by forms or indicating differences by external marks. "It is therefore, the accumulation of forms that should be understood by number 8. This signification is made obvious by the verb '*shmon*,' which means literally, to fatten, to make larger." ("Cosmogony of Moses," 154)

Hieroglyphically, this number reveals that the universal mind was instrumental in mobilizing the creative waters, in drawing constituent parts from its depth, and in rendering them as images or representations of itself, its similitudes in material substance. These similitudes (sons and daughters) were *microcosmic* images of the universal mind, and they characterized or had all the qualities of the universal mind.

Characterizing the attributes of the universal mind into its similitudes encompassed:

- All specifications. That is, all particulars and detailed accounts of Adam's attributes were designated in his similitudes. In other words, the similitudes were minds just like Adam, but they were microcosmic. They were the epitome of Adam in a condensed form, each having in latency all the differentiations of their father Adam, and they were immortal souls like Adam. (Refer to the literal meaning of *Adam* in chapter 1.)
- All classifications or distribution into sets, sorts, ranks, and genus.
  - Sets. That is to say, the souls were placed in their proper classification by type: mankind as opposed to animal kind.
  - Sorts. The souls' denominations were taken into account, and they were sorted out by their genders: male souls and female souls.
  - Rank. The souls were placed in the highest division; mankind's being the highest manifestation of soul life in the physical plane. Psalm 8:5–6 of the Bible ascertains this finding. It states: "God crowned man with glory and honour, has made him to have dominion over the works of his hands, and has put all things under his feet."
  - Genera. Collectively, the souls were considered descending from Adam (the universal mind).
- Describing the souls' evolving qualities by their properties, peculiar qualities, or individual nature
- Giving the souls their proper measure, which ascertained their dimensions (length, breadth, and thickness or depth) and which defined or reduced them to precision
- Assigning the souls with their proper number(s) to express their mathematical magnitude (precise amount) as in counting,

especially (a) given to them to indicate their position (or number) in a group or series or as a mark of identification (as one soul may be given the number one because it was made first, another soul may be given the number two because it was made second, and so on) and (b) used to count the souls in a plurality, as in expressing their total. (i.e.: The number of souls produced may be totaled as 1,000,000,000,000,000[10])

- Giving the souls form
- Giving the souls determinations or boundaries to designate a limit to their extent
- Qualifying any acquirements endowed to the souls
- Giving the souls the ability to adapt (to accommodate, adjust, or conform)

In summary, characterizing the attributes of the universal mind into its similitudes encompassed figuring, defining, forming images of the universal mind, and particularizing or giving individual forms to its images, though embryonic in their state of development. Number eight reveals that the souls grew to a great size. They were fattened and made fruitful, free, and unencumbered to develop to the extent of Adam circumscription. *Mâoth* concurs with this knowledge.

The Hebrew words *iôled banîm w'banôth* validate that the universal mind emanated many souls. Strictly speaking, the production of souls was the embodiment of Adam dividing and infinitely succeeding, with each soul following one another in order. Since the souls were made in the likeness of Adam, and Adam is the universal mind, the souls then constitute the assemblage of all minds.[3] That is to say, Adam became numerous by subdivision, and hence the adage: "the one becoming the many."[4]

Just like Sheth was created to enable the universal mind to build the souls' foundations, other faculties that will be developed (as conveyed throughout Genesis 5) will be added to this assemblage of minds. That is, each mind in the assemblage—each being a *microcosm* of the universal mind—will be endowed with powers to be possessed by the universal mind. This does not mean that humanity (the assemblage of all minds) has the great wisdom possessed by the universal mind from which our minds have proceeded, but it does mean that if we look at ourselves as an extension of the universal mind that we have in us a portion of that great mind.

This is sufficient for our average earthly needs. It constitutes the divine heritage born in us, which controls our bodies in their important functionings and aids us in answering important questions at crucial moments. It supplies us with that essential knowledge necessary to guide us aright in life.

But the small portion of the universal mind in us cannot have the great wisdom possessed by the larger body of the universal mind. Only when we are in attunement with the larger body do we manifest a superior wisdom that enables us to sense all things and to understand. It is like entering a library of reference books covering every subject. The amount of knowledge in each of us is equivalent only to one book of that library; yet when we attune to the library itself (or come into communion with the universal mind), we are like the person in the library, with immediate access to all the books.

SUMMARY

Genesis 5:4 reveals that the energetic, forceful, qualitative, and formative power of the universal mind brought forth the souls of men, and that they bear the resemblance of the universal mind. It conveys that since the universal mind made the souls in its likeness, all existing souls constitute the assemblage of all minds. Each mind in the assemblage being a microcosm of the universal mind is endowed with like powers or faculties possessed by the universal mind. This does not mean that humanity (the assemblage of all minds) has the great wisdom possessed by the universal mind from which our minds have proceeded, but it does mean that if we look at ourselves as an extension of the universal mind that we have in us a portion of that great mind.

★ *PRACTICAL APPLICATION*

Genesis 5:4 reveals that the souls of men bear the resemblance of the universal mind. Therefore, our souls circumscribe the extent of the universal mind in a condensed form. It connotes that we have the power to develop ideas and create—just like the universal mind but in smaller dimensions. This conveys that we are fundamentally creative beings. Our greatest creation is that of building ourselves, our own character. We can make or unmake ourselves by the thoughts we harbor.

Our minds are the master builders of who we are. With certain fundamentals well established as a foundation upon which to build the superstructure of our characters and personalities, we can build in accordance with our individual needs and requirements and yet build strongly because of the proper foundation. For example, if we want to create a noble character, we must exert effort in right thinking by cherishing noble thoughts. The outer manifestations of nobility can only be in accordance with inner changes. As governor of our own thoughts, we hold the key to every situation, and we contain within ourselves that transforming and regenerative agency by which we make ourselves what we will.

CRITICAL THINKING

1. Generating the souls of men required an intricacy of steps. The number eight hundred employed by Moses to explain the event concealed this. What is the underlying meaning of the number eight hundred?

2. What is the meaning of the adage "the one becoming the many"?

3. As part of the assemblage of all minds, how is man viewed?

4. As an extension of the universal mind, humanity is endowed with faculties or powers possessed by the universal mind. How can this endowment of faculties help man?

5. The small portion of the universal mind in man cannot have the great wisdom possessed by the larger body of the universal mind. How can man manifest superior wisdom to enable him to sense all things and to understand?

(Answers in Appendix B)

---

[1] *Creative waters*: the element from which everything draws its nourishment. The ancients regarded it as the female principle of all generation (*The Hebraic Tongue Restored*, 387). They are the fiery androgynous water—also known as *Schamayim*—the source of all elements existing beyond the sphere of the stars (*The Secret Teachings of All Ages*, CLV).

[2] Refer to the figurative meaning of the name *Adam* in chapter 1.

[3] Refer to the literal meaning of the name *Adam* in chapter 1.

[4] Refer to the hieroglyphic meaning of the name *Adam* in chapter 1.

5

THE SOULS OF MEN: SIMILITUDES OF THE UNIVERSAL MIND, PART 2

GENESIS 5:5

- Translation from the King James Version of the Bible: "And all the days that Adam lived were nine hundred and thirty years; and he died."
- The literal English translation as it appears in *The Hebraic Tongue Restored*: "And they were all the days (manifested lights) of Adam (collective man) which he lived-in, nine hundreds of revolving-change; and thirty of revolving change; and he deceased."
- Transliteration from *The Hebraic Tongue Restored*: "Wa-îhîou chol-îmeî Adam âsher-haî theoshah mæôth shanah w-sheloshîm shanah, wa-îamoth."

The following interpretation of Genesis 5:5 is spiritual in nature, not physical.

PROEM

In the previous chapter we learned that the universal mind (Adam) produced the souls of men, and that they were made to develop to the extent of Adam's circumscription. Advancing the souls into a consolidated state to preserve their individuality from loss and keep them in an entire state is next. Genesis 5:5 reveals how this progression ensued and how the universal mind transmuted as a succeeding change under natural laws.

You may have heard the statement, "For every action there is a reaction." The reaction may bring reward or punishment. Cause and effect cannot be severed, for the effect already blooms in the cause. This means that there is a rule of action that enforces a law, the Law of Cause and Effect. It exists as an order in nature by which results follow causes. It denotes consequences that follow one's own actions. To this end, Genesis 5:5 discloses that the antecedent accomplishments of the universal mind (serving as causes) caused a transformation, which changed the universal mind into a different way of being (the effect).

Up to now, chapters 2, 3, and 4 have revealed how the universal mind was first endowed with the male and female principles (intellect and will/volition). This was followed by the production of a faculty that would enable the universal mind to build the groundwork of the souls. Subsequently, the assemblage of souls was produced. At this stage of development, the Hebrew text reveals that the natural progression of the universal mind is to transmute or change from one nature to another. Concealed within the number 930 given in Genesis 5:5 is the knowledge of the various antecedent processes that lead to the transmutation of the universal mind.

UNDERLYING MEANING OF THE NUMBER 930

We will begin our interpretation of the number 930 by analyzing its three components: *theoshah, mæôth,* and *sheloshîm.*

Theoshah (number nine) signifies, literally, lime (a viscous material) and cement. This number draws with it all ideas of cementation, consolidation, restoration, and conservation. It expresses the action of cementing, plastering, or closing carefully. By interpreting each monosyllabic component of the name *theoshah,* we extract additional meaning.

Theoshah reveals that the universal mind gradually metamorphosed the assemblage of souls (before it transmuted). This was a gradual process that consolidated or pressed their loose constituent parts together to preserve their individuality or separate distinct existence from loss and to keep them in an entire state (that is, all parts together). It was the advancing step-by-step cementation, guaranteeing and plastering of the souls. This can be likened to the application of glutinous substances or mortar, which hardens to produce cohesion, and likened to smoothing over any imperfections (the plastering effect). It connotes that the universal mind molded and carefully closed the souls' animated matter. That is to say, the souls quickened following the consolidating and plastering actions of the universal mind. *Mæôth* reveals that these were transitional movements that led the universal mind to establish the souls' kingdom in matter.

Accordingly, *sheloshîm* reveals that the universal mind moved across the circumferential extent and exerted its powers to soften, knead, and make the firm, unyielding, and divided formless matter ductile, which enabled it to unite the qualities of the souls en masse and to develop the collective mind in matter.

CIRCULAR MOVEMENT OF THE UNIVERSAL MIND

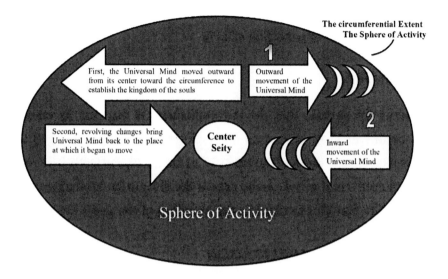

Figure 5.1 above depicts the universal mind moving across its sphere of activity to establish the kingdom of the souls, an outward movement (#1), and subsequently, it shows the universal mind returning to seity, an inward movement (#2).

TRANSMUTATION OF THE UNIVERSAL MIND

The Hebrew word *shanah* reveals that the universal mind underwent universal and ontological revolving changes, passing from one state of development to another while endeavoring to produce Sheth and the immortal souls of men. These changes revolved around a period of activities that once ended brought the universal mind back to its state of seity (or individuality), the state from whence it had begun to move. However, *shanah* discloses that the universal mind was not found at the end of this period in the same state that it was at its beginning. The universal mind had grown in stature by a natural, gradual assimilating process of its newly developed faculties.

The Hebrew word *iamoth* relates that the succeeding change or transmutation[1] was in accord with the Law of Cause and Effect. The accomplishments of the universal mind were causes in relation to its next higher state of seity (the effect).

SUMMARY

Genesis 5:5 reveals that the accomplishments (serving as causes) of the universal mind caused a transformation, which changed the universal mind into a different way of being (the effect). It reveals that the universal mind moved across the circumferential extent and exerted its faculties to develop the kingdom of the souls in matter.

★ PRACTICAL APPLICATION

Genesis 5:5 relates how the universal mind transmuted as a consequence (or effect) of its actions. The Law of Cause and Effect is all-embracing, all-reaching. Every act, conscious or not, brings its effect. When we actuate on our thoughts, we bring upon ourselves consequences, good or bad. If we desire to bring forth good outcomes, we must weave enlightenment and happiness into our thinking practices. Few are aware of this practice, and therefore many people build in pain, suffering, and ignorance.

The task of creating our own future is the inescapable lot of every one. This necessity presents a challenge and a responsibility. Our destiny on earth and in the future lies in our own hands to a very great extent, and no divine intervention may be expected, except that which we earn or deserve through our own actions. We not only have the power to create conditions for ourselves—willfully, deliberately, and with intelligent understanding of what we are doing—but we also have the ability to create unconsciously and unknowingly a great deal of our destiny. "We grow by Law, and cause and effect is absolute and undeviating in the hidden realm of thought."[2]

Each moment, our careers, worldly situations, and conditions are affected by our attitudes of mind, our thinking, and our actions. The thoughts in our minds are what make us. "If we have bad thoughts, pain comes to us as comes the wheel the ox behind us. In purity of thoughts joy follows"[3]—like our own shadow. Therefore, it behooves us to reflect upon our conditions and search diligently for the law upon which our being is established. This will help us to direct our energies with intelligence and to fashion our thoughts to fruitful issues.

CRITICAL THINKING

1. Genesis 5:5 reveals that the universal mind transmuted to a different way of being. Name the cause(s) that produced this effect.
2. What is the underlying meaning of the number 930 as described in Genesis 5:5?
3. How can we make good use of the Law of Cause and Effect in our lives?

(Answers in Appendix B)

---

[1] A successive change led the universal mind to its transmutation, not its death, as written in the Bible, for mind is immortal. (Refer to the figurative meaning of the name *Adam* in chapter 1.)

[2] "As a Man Thinketh" by James Allen.

[3] Ibid.

6

CORPOREAL MAN: ÆNOSH

GENESIS 5:6

- Translation from the King James Version of the Bible: "And Seth lived an hundred and five years, and begat Enos."
- The literal English translation as it appears in *The Hebraic Tongue Restored*: "And he lived, Sheth, five revolving changes and one hundred of revolving change; and he begat Ænosh (corporeal man)."
- Transliteration from *The Hebraic Tongue Restored*: "Wa îhî Sheth hamesh shanîm w-mâth shanah wa-iôled Ænosh."

The following interpretation of Genesis 5:6 is spiritual in nature, not physical.

PROEM

Ancient mystical teachings tell us that man has always been in search of himself, that he desires to know who he is, why he does what he does, and why good and bad things happen to him. The answer to these questions is to be found in man's constitution. Genesis 5:6 covers this subject splendidly. It elucidates upon the physical faculties of corporeal man, which serves to explain man's experiences, happenings, and events.

In the previous chapter, we learned how the universal mind changed into a different way of being after having exerted its faculties to develop the kingdom of souls (the collective mind). This successive change marked the beginning of another period of activity for the universal mind. The manifestation of a new faculty distinguished this new period. This chapter addresses how Moses utilized the number 105 to relate the advent of this new faculty.

UNDERLYING MEANING OF THE NUMBER 105

Let us begin our interpretation of number 105 by examining the two Hebrew names that compose this number: *Hamesh* (number five) and *Mâth* (number one hundred).

Hamesh reveals a movement of contraction and apprehension that results from the five fingers of the hand grasping a thing, pressing tightly and warming it. This is a general envelopment, an inwrapping or covering of all sides. Heat (the exciting or rousing into action) results from the envelopment. The effect of the contractile movement is impressed by the envelopment.

Hamesh is herewith utilized to relate how the universal mind caused the depths of elementary existence to manifest elements (electrons, protons, and other constituent parts). By contractile movements, the universal mind mobilized the creative waters (where the elements of everything that is to exist are held in solution) to make the elements palpable and compact. This enabled the universal mind to draw them from their depth.

Hamesh tells us that the passive and conditional casuality[1] of the universal mind took place enabling it to receive impressions resulting from being in contact with the elements. This influenced the universal mind in fashioning the elements in accordance with the impressions received.

Possessing the faculty Sheth enabled the universal mind to establish the working ground fundamental for the elements to take root and produce.

Further, the Hebrew word *shanîm* and the name *mâth* (number one hundred) reveal that the universal mind passed from one state to another endeavoring to develop the elements to the extent they manifested the new faculty exteriorly. *Shanah* reveals that these were universal and ontological mutations, which caused changes in the nature, essence, qualities, and attributes of the universal mind and it altered it in form. This carries the idea that the universal mind had begun to bring forth its new faculty either in the order of things, or in the order of time relative to its diverse mutations. The Hebrew words *iôled Ænosh* confirm the universal mind emanated its new faculty and that it was named Ænosh (physical faculties).

ÆNOSH

The Hebrew text discloses that *Ænosh* is corporeal man and is considered mutable. This means that corporeal man changes; is capable of being altered in form, qualities, or nature; and consists of material substance. That is, it has a form. Further, the Hebrew text conveys that the name *Ænosh* develops the contradictory ideas of "being" and "nothingness," of "strength" and "weakness," of "virtue" and "vice."

CONTRADICTORY IDEAS

Of *Being* and *Nothingness*

In *being*, corporeal man is endowed with life; he exists in actuality, has existed, may exist or be conceived, and has a mortal existence.

In *nothingness*, corporeal man does not exist, for nothingness negates being. It connotes that corporeal man can exist in a state of annihilation, of being reduced to nothing, of having his identity, his form, his combination of parts or distinctive properties destroyed (through wars, murder, self-destruction or suicide, death, etc.) so that he no longer exists.

Of *Strength* and *Weakness*

In *strength*, corporeal man possesses physical force, power, or energy, such as muscular force or vigor. He may sustain the application of force without breaking or yielding. He has solidity or toughness. He has the power of resistance; the ability to do or to bear; the capacity for exertion—whether physical, intellectual, or moral, such as intensity, power of mind, or intellectual force—and the power of any faculty, such as strength of mind, memory, or judgment. Corporeal man also has the power to express meaning by words, eloquence, and the vigor of style. He has qualities that tend to secure results, and in the fine arts, he has boldness of conceptions or treatments.

In *weakness*, corporeal man exhibits debility, failing, foibles or moral weakness, feebleness, folly, frailty, imbecility, impotence, infirmity, inability, silliness, and stupidity. In weakness, corporeal man shows deficiency in bodily strength (being powerless in operation), inefficaciousness; deficiency in functional energy, activity, or force; and lack of moral or mental strength, vigor, or energy. He is deficient in strength of intellect or judgment and wanting in strength of mind or resolution. He has imperfect mental faculties.

He is foolish and fatuous and has not acquired full confidence or conviction. He is not firmly settled or established, as he wavers, vacillates, and is deficient in steadiness or firmness. He is not able to resist temptation, persuasion, urgency, or the like, and he is easily moved, impressed, or overcome. He exhibits want of discernment, which arises from or is characterized by want of moral courage, self-denial, or determination. He is injudicious, not supported by the force of reason or truth, unsustained, and not founded in right or justice. He is deficient in power or vigor of expression, for he shows weakness of style. He is slight, inconsiderate, little, and infirm. He is debilitated, enervated, invalid, and sickly.

Of *Virtue* and *Vice*

Corporeal man possesses *higher virtues*, *mental virtues*, and *lower virtues of the higher nature*. The *higher virtues* are those of love and the ideals of truth, wisdom, moral excellence, uprightness, rectitude, temperance, charity, bravery, valor, daring, chastity, efficacy, goodness, honesty, integrity, justice, and perfection. We can witness the higher virtues in unselfishness, gentleness, sympathy, compassion, kindness, steadfastness, patience, faith, hope, and reverence.

The *mental virtues* are those of reason, judgment, dispassion, balance, breadth, largeness, liberality of treatment, liberality of thought and sentiment, and freedom from narrowness in opinion.

The *lower virtues of the higher nature* are those of affection, sociability, friendship, generosity, courtesy, courage, prudence, fairness, truthfulness, simplicity, ethics, honor, commitment, duty, and fidelity.

In *vice*, corporeal man indulges in evil habits or conducts, such as moral faults or failings. He participates in particular forms of wickedness or depravity, such as immorality (specifically, the indulgence of impure or degrading appetites or passions), drunkenness, gambling, lewdness, lust, abuse, or any activity that is morally base or impure, sinful, mean, odious, worthless, abject, despicable, low, and profligate. That is, corporeal man is broken or ruined in morals, abandoned to vice, and lost to principles, virtue, or decency. He is vicious, shameless in wickedness, ignorant, unlearned, etc.

Moreover, the Hebrew text conveys that *Ænosh* expresses the instabilities, caducities, and infirmities of temporal (corporeal) man.

INSTABILITIES, CADUCITIES, AND INFIRMITIES OF TEMPORAL (CORPOREAL) MAN

Instabilities include a lack of firm purpose, changeableness, inconstancy, fickleness, and mutability of opinion or conduct. Instability is a characteristic of weak minds.

Caducities are the tendencies of corporeal man (as a mutable being) to fail and to become senile, and decrepit—the broken state of the body produced by decay and the infirmities of age.

Infirmities are the weaknesses, feebleness, debilities, imperfections, failings, and faults of temporal man: He is easy to seduce or entice from the path of rectitude and duty in any manner. It is easy to tempt him and lead him to iniquity, to lead him astray into being variable or transitory—literally as well as figuratively.

Temporal man is mutable and permutable—that is, he is capable of being changed from one state to another through giving up or resigning one position or standing for another. He is capable of being subtracted, of withdrawing from or neglecting duty, of being distracted or drawn apart and separated, of being confused when multiple objects crowd in on the mind and draw the attention different ways.

Temporal man is capable of cheating or defrauding by deception. That is, he is capable of misleading through guile, duplicity, deceit, and trickery. He is capable of being weak, deficient, infirm, and fragile, and he can easily bend. He is not able to resist onset or attack. He is unfit and is easily surmounted or overcome.

He has imperfect mental faculties, is capable of doing wrong, and is not fit or suitable, as he deviates from moral rectitude. He is inequitable, unjust, inaccurate, and erroneous in his beliefs. He is capable of being incorrect, faulty, detrimental, injurious, hurtful, etc.

The Hebrew text also states that *Ænosh* announces a tranquil power, a gentle movement relative to a transient duration. This faculty, says the Hebrew text, lets go, relaxes, and carries to the circumference (the sphere of activity) the contradictory ideas of *being* and *nothingness*, of *strengths* and *weaknesses*, of *virtues* and *vices*—and the instabilities, caducities, and infirmities of temporal man.

A later chapter reveals that another faculty was developed and added to the physical faculties of corporeal man. This other faculty bestows the potential for repentance and contrition (remorse), enabling corporeal man to exonerate himself for wrongdoing.

ADAM'S MICROCOSM (3/10)

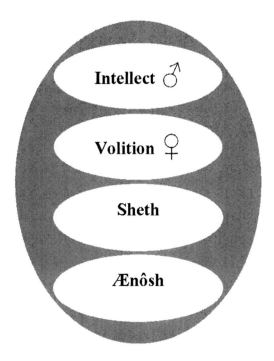

Figure 6.1 above shows that the faculties of Adam within his microcosm are now composed of intellect (male principle), volition/ will (female principle), *Sheth* (Adam's power to frame the foundation of the soul), and *Ænôsh*, (Adam's physical faculties, corporeal man).

At this stage of development, Adam's microcosm is only partially evolved and is therefore imperfect. When the microcosm is fully evolved, it will be as perfect as his macrocosm, *Ælohîm*.

SUMMARY

Genesis 5:6 reveals the advent of the physical faculties of corporeal man, which serves to explain man's experiences, happenings, and events.

Further, it relates that *Ænosh* is corporeal man, is considered mutable, and it develops the contradictory ideas of *being* and *nothingness*, of *strength* and *weakness*, and of *virtue* and *vice*.

In addition, it discloses that *Ænosh* expresses the instabilities, caducities, and infirmities of temporal man, and it announces a tranquil power, a gentle movement relative to a transient duration.

★ PRACTICAL APPLICATION

Throughout history, we find that man exhibits characteristics of goodness and moral excellence. We have also observed that he exhibits the impulse or desire to do harm, cheat, lie, and be perverse, turning from the right or the truth. Genesis 5:6 has revealed that man is endowed with life; that he can exist in a state of annihilation; that he possesses strengths, weaknesses, virtues, and vices; and that as a temporal man he has instabilities, caducities, and infirmities.

A question may now arise: how does man overcome his frailties and develop his inherent virtues?

There comes a time in man's evolution when he becomes extremely dissatisfied with his faults and limitations and begins to aspire for a higher way of life. He begins to conform to rules of right and develops a sense of duty, virtues, and principles of rectitude. As he continues to raise his consciousness, he begins to see a vast and universal harmony that helps him to recognize the underlying principle of life as a rhythmic pattern of unity—and to see his individual note as but one in a symphonic whole. He begins to alter the inherited and acquired conditions about him to create a new life for himself.

This task of creating his own life is the inescapable lot of every individual. It presents a challenge and a responsibility, which he accepts and recognizes as a consequence or the harvesting effects of his actions. He understands that the limitations imposed upon him by his physical inheritance and background are only apparent, and he endeavors to change and modify these conditions consciously, overcoming and correcting the errors he has made, thereby placing himself on the path of swift unfoldment.

CRITICAL THINKING

1. Ancient mystical teachings tell us that man has always been in search of himself. He desires to know who he is, why he does what he does, and why good and bad things happen to him. Where may man find his answers?
2. What is the constitution of man?
3. The number 105 used in Genesis 5:6 conveys how the universal mind rendered the elements of a new faculty manifest and obvious. Which faculty is Genesis 5:6 relating to?
4. What is the meaning of the name *Ænosh*?
5. According to the Hebrew text, corporeal man is considered mutable. Why?
6. What does corporeal man consists of?
7. The name *Ænosh* develops contradictory ideas. Name them.
8. Corporeal man may exist in a state of annihilation. Why?
9. Corporeal man has the capacity for exertion, whether physical, intellectual, or moral. These are examples of _____ (fill in the blank).
10. Corporeal man is foolish and fatuous. He has not acquired full confidence or conviction. He is not firmly settled or established. He wavers and vacillates and is deficient in steadiness or firmness. These are examples of _____ (fill in the blank).

11. Name the three groupings of corporeal man's virtues.

12. Temporal man is notorious for three things. Name them.

(Answers in Appendix B)

[1.] The passive and conditional casuality of the universal mind is a power that influences and moves the mind, makes impressions and have dominion.

7

FOUNDATIONS FOR THE SOULS OF MEN: SHETH'S SIMILITUDES, PART 1

GENESIS 5:7

- Translation from the King James Version of the Bible: "And Seth lived after he begat Enos eight hundred and seven years and begat sons and daughters."
- The literal English translation as it appears in *The Hebraic Tongue Restored*: "And he lived, Sheth, after the causing him to beget that same Ænosh, seven revolving changes, and eight hundreds of revolving change; and he begat sons and daughters (a flocking throng of issued beings)."
- Transliteration from *The Hebraic Tongue Restored*: "Wa-îhî Sheth âhareî hôlîd-ô-æth Ænosh Shebah shanîm w'shemoneh mæoth shanah wa-iôled banîm w-banôth."

The following interpretation of Genesis 5:7 is spiritual in nature, not physical.

PROEM

We learned in chapter 3 how the universal mind began the process of building up the souls' foundations by first developing its own faculty

57

to enable it to create the foundations. Further, we learned that the universal mind named this faculty *Sheth*.

In this chapter, we are told that *Sheth* is activated to empower the universal mind to generate the souls' foundations or groundwork on which their various vehicles of consciousness—mental, emotional, astral, and physical vestures, also known as "coats of skin" (Gen. 3:21)—can be built upon. This is likened to the foundation of a house, which must be built before its walls can be erected.

FOUNDATIONS FOR THE SOULS OF MEN: BEGINNING STAGES

The Hebrew words *âhareî* and *hôlid* in Genesis 5:7 convey the related events leading to the formation of the foundations.

Âhareî reveals that the universal mind extracted elements from elementary existence as the preliminary step to making similitudes of its faculty *Sheth*, which is the blueprint or archetypal model used to build the similitudes or foundations of the souls. *Âhareî* further reveals that the universal mind compressed and confined the elements from free movement to give them a definite form or expression that was compacted and centralized.

Centralization of the elements caused an effluvium to appear. These were ethereal spiritual emanations of the foundations demonstrating their power of being.

Hôlid reveals that even though the foundations did not yet exist, they were found nevertheless to have the power to exist. It necessitated that the universal mind pass the effluvium from one nature to another in an eccentric movement designed to extend, rise, and unfold the effluvium in all directions within its area of activity. Unfolding the effluvium bound their nonbeing to being. It was the beginning of building the solid grounds on which the vestures of the souls would rest. Hence, the foundations began to be cemented and knitted; that is, they began to be framed, raised, or shaped into particular forms. Number 807 and the Hebrew word *shanîm* relate how this unfoldment took place.

UNDERLYING MEANING OF THE NUMBER 807

We will begin our interpretation of the number 807 by examining the three names that compose this number: *shebah*, *shemoneh*, and *mœôth*.

Shebah (number seven) gives the ideas of complement, accomplishment, consummation of things, the fullness of times, complete restitution, cyclic fullness, and a return to the place from which one has departed. Added to these ideas are every kind of curve or inversion of cycle—a change of order so that the last (the mind incarnated in the physical) becomes the first (in the ascending ladder), and the first (the soul) becomes last, indicating a turning or change in the descending and ascending order of the mind and soul. Figure 7.1 below depicts these changes.

THE INVERSION OF CYCLE

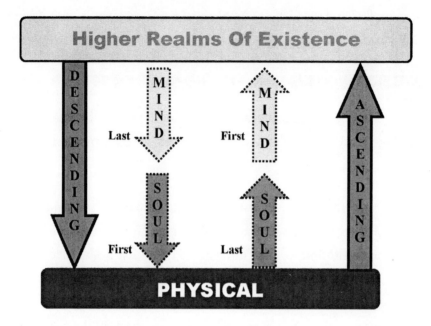

Shebah reveals that the universal mind began to unfold the effluvium by fructifying and producing simple appearances (qualities of the foundations) that rose from spontaneous movements within the universal mind. This is indicative of something that was not yet visible or obvious but that tended from the center (the universal mind) to the circumference (the sphere of activity), and back to the center, likened to projecting one's thoughts toward some place and then returning one's thinking to objectivity. *Shebah* reveals that the foundations' qualities were not ready for their growth and development; nor had they reached their point of departure, because the simple appearances were just interior movements within the universal mind. That is to say, the universal mind foresaw or was cognizant of the gradual progress, of passing the qualities from one state of development to another and finally entering matter.

INVOLUTING THE FOUNDATIONS IN MATTER

Shanîm reveals that the universal mind proceeded to advance the qualities into matter. *Shebah* discloses it necessitated precipitating the qualities with steep descent into matter. These were harsh, rigorous, exacting, inordinate, and vehement movements that caused the qualities of the foundations to involute into material substance. Following their involution, *shemoneh* (number eight) reveals that the qualities of the foundations were made to resemble the faculty *Sheth* and that it encompassed all particulars and detailed accounts of its attributes. All specifications were included. That is to say, Sheth's similitudes (symbolically known as the sons and daughters of Seth in the Bible) were to be the solid ground to which the perceptible qualities of the souls would inhere. Their circumscriptive extent was classified into sets, sorts, ranks, and genera:

- Sets: the foundations were classified by type, made part of the souls of men and not of any other soul life (animals).
- Sorts: the foundations were classified by their gender as male and female foundations.
- Ranks: the foundations were placed in the highest division—mankind's—which is the highest manifestation of soul life on earth.
- Genera: collectively, the foundations were considered to resemble Sheth, and they were differentiated from any other faculty possessed by the universal mind.

Shemoneh conveys that the foundations' circumscriptive extent included describing them by their properties (their inherent qualities), measuring them to ascertain their dimensions (length, breadth, and thickness or depth), which defined or reduced them to precision, and giving them their proper number(s) to:

- Express their mathematical magnitude (precise amount), as in counting;
- Indicate their position (or number) in a group or series or as a mark of identification;
- Count the number of foundations in a plurality, as expressing their total.

Shemoneh further reveals that the foundations were given boundaries, limiting their extent. They were given forms. Endowments (intellect, knowledge, and consciousness of all truth) were fitted. They were qualified to exercise their function. And, they were given the ability to adapt or conform to the souls' uplifting endeavors.

In short, *shemoneh* makes known that the universal mind particularized the souls' foundations by forming models of its faculty *Sheth*. This accomplishment gave the foundations a separate or distinct existence. However, their existence had not reached their point of perfection or completeness for they were in their embryonic state, tending in the direction in which the desires of the universal mind worked or moved. *Shemoneh* reveals that they grew to a great number and were free and unencumbered to develop to the extent of Sheth's circumscription.

Mæoth (number one hundred) discloses that the desire of the universal mind to extend, dilate, and manifest the foundations exteriorly was a sympathetic movement, a reciprocal action in accord with divine laws, and a transitional movement that led the universal mind to mutate repeatedly.

The Hebrew word *shanah* reveals these mutations were universal and ontological. They changed the nature, essence, qualities, and attributes of the universal mind and altered it in form enabling it to bring forth the foundations.

EMANATING THE FOUNDATIONS

The Hebrew words *iôled banîm w-banôth* confirm the universal mind emanated (begat) a great multitude of male and female foundations resembling its faculty Sheth, though embryonic in their state of development. They were the same as Sheth, designed to provide a solid ground to which the perceptible qualities of the souls (mental, emotional, astral, and physical vestures) would inhere.

SHETH DEPICTING THE FOUNDATION OF THE SOUL

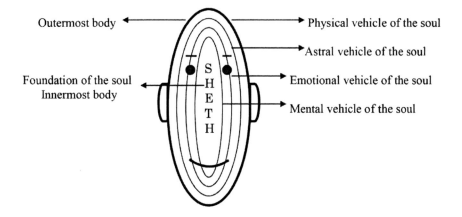

Figure 7.2 above depicts Sheth as the groundwork or foundation, with the mental, emotional, astral, and physical vestures of the soul resting upon it on all sides. As a foundation, Sheth is also known as the *cognitional or causal body* (sphere) of the soul. Sheth is the vehicle of the soul in the Higher Mind by which truth is known. Sheth is the innermost habitat of the soul and is composed of intellection associated with the organs of perception. This gives the soul its first conception of individuality.

To Sheth are attached the vehicles of the personality (mental, emotional, astral, and physical bodies) to function on the lower planes of existence.

The *mental vesture* is sensorial and is the body of the lower mind—the lower mental that sees with the eyes of the mind but perceives through the senses. It is composed of mind stuff or mental matter, which constitutes the materials of all intellectually active qualities. It is associated with the organs of action. This gives the individual soul its powers of thought and judgment.

The *emotional vesture* is the vehicle of feeling and will/volition. It is composed of material denser than mind stuff but thinner than ether.

The *astral vesture* is the instrument by which desires and lower emotions and sensations function. It conserves the principle of bodily vital forces and is the medium between the superphysical and the physical body.

The *physical body* is the outermost vesture of the soul. It is the tangible body of the senses, composed of solid, liquid, and gaseous materials, and is the vehicle of self-expression in the material world. It is the thickest, weightiest instrument of awareness and action. It is the body of flesh, the passive instrument of the soul. It has no life on its own.

SUMMARY

Genesis 5:7 reveals that the universal mind brought forth the souls' foundation on which their various vehicles of consciousness could be built upon. Further, it reveals the foundations resembled Sheth, a faculty of the universal mind. By forming models of Sheth, the universal mind gave the souls' foundations a separate or distinct existence.

★ *PRACTICAL APPLICATION*

Genesis 5:7 conveys that our souls have been given a foundation or solid ground to support our various vehicles of consciousness (mental, emotional, astral, and physical). We learned in chapter 3 that this foundation houses within it the intellect, knowledge, and consciousness of all the truth inherited from the consciousness of Ælohîm, which the universal mind possesses. Ancient esoteric teachings tell us that to access these truths, man must first access his Higher Mind, "where the enduring and real and the archetypal and perfect abide" (GAG, 360).

Further, the teachings tell us that to reach the Higher Mind we must tarry in abstract thinking and maintain our thoughts in the world of Ideas. There, the interaction of ideas brings impressions of mystical beauty down into the brain of the meditator, and the higher emotions into the emotional body. The teachings state that ideas and higher emotions are the most powerful rulers of the Higher Mind when the will is in accord with them. Therefore, the dynamic power of our will (the female principle within us) must be put into operation. We must will and act until access to the Higher Mind (the mind that comprehends all) is achieved.

Accessing the Higher Mind is an evolutionary process that first presents itself as an upward aspiration, a vague and almost unconscious unrest and dissatisfaction at present conditions. The lower mind, being allied with desires and lower emotions, finds it difficult to relinquish these inferior motives, but once they are relinquished and we accept the ideals and higher emotions in place of the lower attachments, we are home free. Here in the Higher Mind, the lower emotions are transmuted into higher emotions, and our indwelling soul evolves as our lower nature falls away.

CRITICAL THINKING

1. In this chapter, we learned that the universal mind brought forth the souls' foundation. For what purpose?
2. What are the souls vehicles of consciousness?
3. _____ is another word used interchangeably with *foundation* or *groundwork*.
4. Genesis 5:7 reveals the related events leading to the formation of the souls' foundations. Relate the events.
5. As a foundation, Sheth is also known as the _____ or _____ _____ of the soul.
6. What gives the soul its first conception of individuality?
7. The mental vesture of the soul is said to be sensorial. It sees with the eyes of the mind but perceives through what organs?
8. Feeling and volition are part of which vesture?
9. Which vesture conserves the principle of the bodily vital forces?
10. The physical body is composed of three substances. Name them.
11. The number 807 used in Genesis 5:7 reveals the details of the foundations' construction. What precipitated their advancement?
12. What action of the universal mind gave the foundations of the souls their separate or distinct existence?

(Answers in Appendix B)

8

FOUNDATIONS FOR THE SOULS OF MEN: SHETH'S SIMILITUDES, PART 2

GENESIS 5:8

- Translation from the King James Version of the Bible: "And all the days of Seth were nine hundred and twelve years: and he died."
- The literal English translation as it appears in *The Hebraic Tongue Restored*: "And they were all the days (manifested lights) of Sheth, two and one ten of revolving-change, and nine hundreds of revolving change; and he deceased."
- Transliteration from *The Hebraic Tongue Restored*: "Wa îhîou chol îmeî Sheth shethîm heshereh shanah, w-theshah mæôth shanah, wa-îamoth."

The following interpretation of Genesis 5:8 is spiritual in nature, not physical.

PROEM

In the previous chapter we learned that the foundations or causal bodies of the souls were brought forth and that their existence had not reached their point of perfection, for they were in their embryonic state, tending in the direction in which the desire of the universal mind worked or moved. It makes sense that their progression should follow. This is precisely what Genesis 5:8 reveals. It discloses how the boundaries, designations, definitions, dispositions, and measures of the foundations were influenced, and how this period of activity was a transition that caused the universal mind to transform into a different way of being. The underlying meaning of the number 912 given in this verse elucidates upon these activities.

UNDERLYING MEANING OF THE NUMBER 912

To find the underlying meaning of the number 912, it is necessary to separately interpret the Hebrew names composing this number: *shethîm*, *heshereh*, *theshah*, and *mæôth*.

Shethîm (number two) contains all ideas of:

- mutation
- transition
- passing from one state to another
- redundancy (superabundance)

Thus the name of this number conveys diversity, change, and variation. Therefore, number two makes known to us the redundant changes undergone by the foundations as they passed from one state to another, evolving into precise forms. That is to say, the prototypal ideas of Sheth were formed and nursed, as it were, or prepared for their reflection downward unto the lower planes. This preparation required direction and government. *Heshereh* reveals this.

Heshereh (number ten) represents:

- aggregative and reforming powers or formative energy
- natural forces unfolding and acting
- congregation of power proper and elementary motive force
- every formation by *aggregation* in order to make, direct, and govern every motive principle or that which incites to action or moves the will

Thus *heshereh* reveals that the aggregative and reforming powers of the universal mind acted upon the foundations in the following fashion. The foundations were conformed by the *aggregation* of elements. They were the consequence of an intelligent movement or plan formed in advance by the *will* of the universal mind (its female principle). By its *will* or *volitive faculty*, the universal mind did the things it conceived to be in its power: thence, a work (it fashioned the elements), a composition (it arranged the elements), and a creation (it fabricated the foundations).

The universal mind assembled its work by using its *aggregative* power and composed its arrangements by using its power to *make*. *Heshereh* further reveals that the universal mind liberated its creation conformable to universal harmony and restricted to regulations according to just and upright divine laws. These laws possessed in them a proper and determining rectilinear movement of progression and renewal, which enabled the universal mind to reestablish, transform, and regenerate the foundations as they converged at the circumference, the creative area of activity. It is here, at the creative area of activity, that the aggregative and reforming power of the universal mind unfolded and acted upon the souls' foundations.

The progression of the foundations was made evident as they underwent repeated mutations. The Hebrew word *shanah* ascertains it. Mutation is a process of changing, of altering in form and in qualities. *Theshah* (number nine) discloses these changes effected the boundaries, the designations, the definitions, the arrangements, and the measures of the foundations. In other words, the foundations were transformed (metamorphosed). It denotes a gradual process that consolidated their loose constituent parts to preserve their separate distinct existence from loss and to keep them in an entire state. That is, the universal mind molded and carefully closed their animated matter, which caused the foundations to quicken, an outcome from the consolidating actions of the universal mind. This is likened to the alterations that an insect undergoes before it becomes a butterfly. All the changes which are undergone by a butterfly in passing from the fecundated ovum to the imago, or perfect insect, constitute its development, each change, from ovum to larva, from larva to pupa, and from pupa to imago, constituting a metamorphosis.

The quickening effect upon the foundations hastened their continuity. *Mœôth* (the last component of the number 912) reveals that this was a transitional movement that led the universal mind to transmute.

TRANSMUTATION OF THE UNIVERSAL MIND

The Hebrew word *shanah* reveals that the transmutation occurred in cyclic changes. These successive changes revolved around this particular period of activities, which once ended returned the universal mind to its state of seity from whence it had begun to move. *Shanah* discloses that the universal mind was not found at the end of this period in the same state that it was at its beginning. The Hebrew word *îamoth* conveys that the universal mind had transformed into a different way of being, the result of having accomplished the aim to which its exertions, intentions, and designs pointed. This succeeding change came under the Law of Cause and Effect. Sheth was the faculty that operated as an "efficient cause" or reason that impelled the universal mind to produce corporeal man and to develop the foundations of the souls (the effect).

SUMMARY

Genesis 5:8 reveals how the progression of the souls' foundations was made evident as they underwent mutations, transformation, and animation. Further, it reveals how the universal mind transformed as a succeeding change that came under the Law of Cause and Effect.

★ PRACTICAL APPLICATION

Genesis 5:8 reveals that the congregation of power within the universal mind unfolds and acts, which enables it to govern that which incites to action. The Kabbalah teaches that the emotions, which are the embodiment of will/volition, provide the power to incite to action. It teaches that once we release our thoughts, our volitive faculty is agitated by our emotions to do the things our minds have conceived. That is to say, by the will of our minds, thoughts are fashioned and created in material substance.

To fashion and create in material substance, the emotion of *desire* plays an important role. This means that the astral plane comes into play as a field or medium for the desires of our mind to pass through into the physical. "Life in the physical plane is a mental directive agency from the astral plane, which uses the forces of the physical plane to build up structure according to its pattern of growth." (GAG, 78) Since thoughts are structured according to their nature, it behooves us to choose what we think about.

We have the freedom to choose our thoughts under all kinds of circumstances and feelings, and under the stress and force of all kinds of motives. We find ourselves having to choose, and choosing—the right things or the wrong—go straight onward or turn aside, giving proof of what is in us: the inmost bias and inclination of our character, the use we make of our freedom, and our strength and mastery over ourselves. Our acts are the result of our thinking. Therefore, by structuring constructive thoughts, we can make our Higher Self govern our lower self; we can make our weaker and poorer and baser wishes yield to our nobler will.[1]

CRITICAL THINKING

1. Number ten in Genesis 5:8 tells us that the foundations were a consequence of an intelligent movement formed in advanced by the universal mind. What gave the universal mind the power to plan in advance?
2. Why did the foundations of the souls converged at the creative area of activity?
3. Number nine relates that the universal mind metamorphosed the souls' foundations. What does this convey?

(Answers in Appendix B)

---

[1] Source: *Dictionary Of All Scriptures And Myths*, 361

9

INVADING FORCE OF THE UNIVERSAL MIND: KAINAN

GENESIS 5:9

- Translation from the King James Version of the Bible: "And Enos lived ninety years, and begat Cainan."
- The literal English translation as it appears in *The Hebraic Tongue Restored*: "And he lived, Ænosh, nine-tens of revolving change, and he begat the self-sameness of Kainan, general invading."
- Transliteration from *The Hebraic Tongue Restored*: "Wa îhî Ænosh thishehîm shanah wa-iôled æth-Keînan."

The following interpretation of Genesis 5:9 is spiritual in nature, not physical.

PROEM

Let us begin this chapter by talking about the law of periodicity or having periods of recurrence—that is, having cycles performing in equal times or things taking place at fixed intervals, such as the periodical production of faculties as conveyed throughout chapter 5 of the Genesis account.

We learned in chapter 3 that the universal mind brought forth Sheth, the faculty that enabled it to frame the foundations (or causal bodies) of the immortal souls of men. This was followed by the production of souls, and then by the transformation of the universal mind, indicating that a period of activity had ended and another had begun. Throughout chapter 5, the beginning of a new period is marked by the bringing forth of a new faculty, and the ending by the transformation of the universal mind into a different way of being.

Following Sheth, the emanation of Ænosh (corporeal man) marked the beginning of new period. The production of causal bodies or foundations came afterward, and this was followed by the transformation of the universal mind, indicating that another period of activity had ended.

Now, a new faculty is due to come forth. Genesis 5:9 reveals that Ænosh enables the universal mind to beget this new power, which is invading, compressive, decisive and agglomerative or repressive. Its name is *Kainan.*

This new faculty will enable the universal mind to carry out more complex tasks. It is likened to a child who first develops his faculty of walking before he can develop his faculty of running, or his speech before his ability to sing a melody. Each succeeding faculty the child develops is followed by a more complex faculty that is capable of doing more. The child's ability to walk, run, speak, and sing is within his being, and his mind directs his movements of walking, running, speaking, and singing. In like manner, the universal mind (Adam) directs the movement of its developing faculties. Each faculty, once developed, gives the universal mind the ability to beget other faculties, which makes the universal mind capable of carrying out more complex tasks.

Genesis 5:9 makes known that the task at hand is to develop a medium through which anything can be done or carried out, a force that will serve to manifest all particular manifestations of individual being. This force will be the invading and compressive, decisive and agglomerative (repressive) power that enables the universal mind to infringe and encroach upon unformed matter (matter suitable to be put in action), and to hold possession of the centralization power that combines and concentrates parts into a whole. This in turn will enable the universal mind to provide the means to attain the souls' material existence, as a natural process of involuting or wrapping them into their vestures—their mental, emotional, astral, and physical vehicles of consciousness.

The Hebrew word *îhî* in Genesis 5:9 reveals that the universal mind began the process of developing its invading force by its impulsions upon elementary existence to render elements (electrons, protons, and other constituent parts) manifest and obvious. *Îhî* reveals that manifesting these elements enabled the universal mind to become conscious of its faculty *Ænosh* being utilized to form the new faculty. The Hebrew word *thishehîm* (number ninety) elaborates further.

UNDERLYING MEANING OF THE NUMBER 90

To develop an understanding of the number ninety, its Hebrew name *thishehîm* must be divided into its simplest components (*thi-thsh-thish-eh-h-hi-im*) and examined in succession.

Thishehîm reveals that the elements to build the invading force were passed from one state of development to another influenced by the interaction that exist between the universal mind and matter, that is, by the creative and multiplying function that occurs in the world of mind and matter.

Interacting with matter was a violent movement, necessitating the universal mind to exert great force upon matter to consolidate and press the elements together to preserve them from loss and to keep them in an entire state. Consolidating the elements enabled the universal mind to mold and carefully close the growth of its developing faculty. Advancing this growth was a goad or an impelling force that incited the universal mind to haste the pace to universalize the developing faculty.

KAINAN: THE GENERAL INVADING
FORCE OF THE UNIVERSAL MIND

The process of universalizing the developing faculty caused the universal mind to undergo universal and ontological mutations. The Hebrew word *shanah* reveals that these mutations changed the nature, essence, qualities, and attributes of the universal mind. It altered the universal mind in form, thereby enabling it to bring forth the existence of its new faculty: a medium that would provide the means to produce vehicles of consciousness enabling the souls to attain material existence. This medium is called *Kainan.*

The Hebrew text discloses that Kainan is the universal mind's general invading force that infringes, encroaches on, falls on, seizes, or generally usurps and holds possession of something.

Kainan is *Kain* extended and diluted. Its force, which consisted in a violent centralization, has diminished in proportion to its extent. Here, the universal mind reproduced a Kain (Cain). That is, it reproduced a strong, mighty faculty that lies in the center and assumes and assimilates to itself. Although *Kainan* may simply be the word *Kain*— to which Moses added the augmentative final *-an*—it is very necessary that there should be preserved in the posterity of Sheth the same nature that it has in its own. *Kainan* is the universal mind's general usurping and invading power that seizes and holds possession of that power.

Kainan is a repressive force that subdues or restrains. It holds back, and it gives the means to attain an end. It is the directing, convulsive, and violent force of the universal mind that serves to manifest all particular manifestations of individual being.

Further, the Hebrew text discloses that possessing the faculty Kainan enables the universal mind to designate that which is indefinite, vague, indeterminate, and unformed—such as matter suitable to be put into action, or the mechanical movement that acts upon it and upon the obtuse, vague, and blind but irresistible force that leads it.

Moreover, the text discloses that the universal mind uses Kainan as the medium through which anything is done or carried out.

In short, Kainan is the universal mind's compressive and decisive power, the agglomerative or repressive force that gives the means to attain material existence in matter that is not yet formed but is suitable to be put into action—that is, to produce, particularize, or individualize existence proper.

ADAM'S MICROCOSM (4/10)

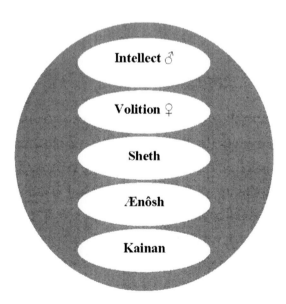

Figure 9.1 above shows the faculties of the universal mind within its microcosm are now composed of intellect (male principle), volition/

will (female principle), Sheth (Adam's power to frame the foundation of the soul), Ænosh (Adam's physical faculties, corporeal man), and Kainan (Adam's general invading force).

SUMMARY

This chapter reveals that the beginning of a new period of activity is marked by the bringing forth of a new faculty, and the ending, by the transformation of the universal mind into another way of being.

Genesis 5:9 reveals that another period of activity had begun by the advent of a new faculty. This new faculty is called Kainan, the general invading force of the universal mind. It enables the universal mind (Adam) to designate that, which is indefinite, vague, indeterminate, and unformed, such as matter suitable to be put into action. Further, it enables the universal mind to take possession of the centralization power that combines and concentrates parts into a whole, thereby supplying the means to attain the material existence of souls, as a natural process of wrapping them into their vestures.

★ PRACTICAL APPLICATION

Genesis 5:9 reveals that the invading, encroaching force of the universal mind gives the means to attain the material existence of things. It reveals that this force works upon unformed matter that is suitable to be put into action, which is likened to molding clay. Clay has no form before the fingers of the artist give it the desired form. In this analogy, clay would be considered unformed matter suitable to be put into action by the fingers of the artist (the medium).

In like manner, we can apply this principle to personal acquisitions. For example, we can mentally mold our thoughts and form images of things that may be felt, weighed, or seen, or that may in any way be known to have physical properties (a house, a garden, clothing, furniture, household items, etc.).

Mental forms are the unformed matter within the mind of the thinker, and it is matter suitable to be put into action. The release of our will or volitive faculty (the medium) activates these mental forms for their manifestation in material substance. That is, we can apply our energy (volitive faculty) as the force (the medium) to obtain the desired end.

CRITICAL THINKING

1. According to the law of periodicity, things take place at fixed intervals, such as the periodical production of faculties as conveyed throughout Genesis 5. How many faculties have been endowed to and brought forth from the universal mind thus far? Name them.

2. What determines that a new period of activity has begun in the universal mind?

3. What determines the ending of a period of activity in the universal mind?

4. What happens to the universal mind before it emanates a new faculty?

5. What happens when the universal mind mutates?

6. Genesis 5:9 reveals the advent of a new faculty. What faculty did the universal mind bring forth?

7. What is the name of this new faculty?

8. Developing Kainan was a goad that incited a hastier pace to universalize its material development. What does this statement convey?

9. The Hebrew text discloses that Kainan is the _____ to attain the souls' _____ _____.

10. As a convulsive and violent force of the universal mind, Kainan serves to manifest what?

11. As a compressive and decisive power, and as an agglomerative or repressive force, Kainan gives the means to attain material existence. Where does this material existence take place?

(Answers in Appendix B)

10

PHYSICAL FACULTIES OF CORPOREAL MAN: ÆNOSH'S SIMILITUDES, PART 1

GENESIS 5:10

- Translation from the King James Version of the Bible: "And Enos lived after he begat Cainan eight hundred and fifteen years and begat sons and daughters."
- The literal English translation as it appears in *The Hebraic Tongue Restored*: "And he lived, Ænôsh, after the causing him to beget the selfsameness of Kainan, five and one tens of revolving change, and eight hundreds of revolution, and he begat sons and daughters (many issued offspring)."
- Transliteration from *The Hebraic Tongue Restored*: "Wa-îhî Ænôsh âhoreî hôlid-ô æth-Keînan hamesh heshereh shanah w'shemoneh mæôth shanah wa-iôled banîm w-banôth."

The following interpretation of Genesis 5:10 is spiritual in nature, not physical.

PROEM

In this chapter we are told how the universal mind brought forth the physical faculties of corporeal man and how it utilized its invading force

(*Kainan*) as a medium to attain their material existence. The intricacies of steps taken to produce the physical faculties are revealed below.

ELEMENTARY MANIFESTATION
OF PHYSICAL FACULTIES

The Hebrew text reveals that the impulsions of the universal mind on elementary existence rendered elements (electrons, protons, and other constituent ingredients) manifest and obvious and that manifesting these elements was the beginning step to building the physical faculties of corporeal man.

The Hebrew word *âhoreî* reveals that evolving the physical faculties required that the universal mind centralize the elements, which demanded effort, care, and fatigue. This conveys that the universal mind labored to keep the elements in a state of balance, so that they remained in equilibrium, even, uniform, and alike in state, magnitude, dimensions, degree, and the like.

Further, *âhoreî* reveals that the effort exerted upon the elements compressed, stabilized, and confined them, preventing free movement. This enabled the universal mind to set and to give them definite forms or expressions that were compacted and centralized.

Centralization brought reconciliation (stasis) of the seeming contrarieties or antagonistic forces (i.e., centripetal[1] and centrifugal[2] forces) surrounding the elements. These were forces whose united action caused the elements to revolve around a central point, making consistent or congruous things apparently opposed or inconsistent. This furnishes the idea of the perfect repose that results after a thing has been agitated contrarily for a long time, the point of immobile equilibrium that, when attained, produces stasis. It is likened to a state of rest produced when two forces acting upon a body are equally opposed to each other that the body remains at rest. Although one of those forces would move the body if it acted alone, those forces are said to be in equilibrium, equally balanced.

Centralization of the elements caused an effluvium, or ethereal spiritual emanations of the physical faculties. The Hebrew word *hôlid* reveals that this effluvium was evidence of the faculties' potential life or power of being. Their power of being manifested when the universal mind passed the effluvium from one nature to another in an eccentric movement designed to unfold the physical faculties in all directions within its sphere of activity—east, west, north, south, southeast, southwest, northeast, northwest, and depth. This required that the universal mind execute its power of acting and dominion over the universal quaternary[3] and over its faculty Kainan to attain the material existence of the physical faculties in matter that was not yet formed. The number 815 given in Genesis 5:10 recounts the activities given above and elucidates further.

UNDERLYING MEANING OF THE NUMBER 815

To obtain the knowledge hidden within the number 815, we must examine individually the Hebrew names that compose this number: *hamesh, heshereh, shemoneh,* and *mœôth.*

Hamesh (number five) reveals that the universal mind exerted great force upon elementary existence to render elements manifest and obvious. This connotes that the universal mind was instrumental in mobilizing the creative waters (where the elements of everything that is to exist are held in solution) to make the elements palpable and compact, and subsequently to draw them from their depth.

It reveals that the passive and conditional casuality of the universal mind enabled it to receive impressions (images, representations of the physical faculties) arising from being in contact with the elements.

This triggered its plastic power to begin to fashion the elements in accordance with the impressions received.

In consequence of an intelligent movement or plan formed in advance by its will (female principle), *heshereh* (number ten) reveals that the universal mind descended onto its sphere of activity to involute the elements into the physical, low-down, and degraded sentient existence (the negative, material polarity of Spirit) where they were given physical reality, superficies, exterior forms, growth, and material development. Their material development conformed to universal harmony and they were restricted to regulations according to divine laws. These laws possessed in them a proper and determining rectilinear movement of progression and renewal, which reestablished, transformed, and regenerated the evolving physical faculties as they developed into precise forms.

The process of evolving the physical faculties brought forth changes in the universal mind. The Hebrew word *shanah* reveals that the universal mind underwent universal and ontological mutations, which caused changes in the nature, essence, qualities, and attributes of the universal mind. It altered the universal mind in form connoting the forthcoming emanations of the physical faculties.

MATERIAL DEVELOPMENT OF PHYSICAL FACULTIES

Shemoneh (number eight) conveys that the universal mind universalized the evolving physical faculties throughout the circumferential extent (its entire sphere of activity). This was a movement by which the universal mind was instrumental in mobilizing the passive and creative waters in order to draw elements, and subsequently, to render them into images, representations, or similitudes of Ænosh (the physical faculties of corporeal man) in material substance. This rendering conveys that the similitudes (the symbolical sons and daughters of Ænosh) circumscribed the extent of Ænosh. They characterized all specifications or detailed description of Ænosh's attributes, such as possessing the contradictory ideas of "being and nothingness," "strengths and weaknesses," and "virtues and vices." (Refer to the meaning of *Ænosh* in chapter 6.)

All physical faculties (Ænosh attributes) were distributed into sets, sorts, ranks, and classes. They were classified by type that corresponded to the souls of men, not to any other soul life (animals). They were sorted by gender: male physical faculties and female physical faculties. They were ranked or placed in the highest division—mankind—as opposed to animal kind. They were classed collectively as the resemblance of Ænosh; that is, they were differentiated from any other faculties possessed by the universal mind.

The circumscription of the physical faculties (Ænôsh's similitudes) encompassed:

- describing them by their properties or peculiar qualities: for instance, physical strengths, mental strengths, vices, weaknesses, or virtues
- measuring them to ascertain their dimensions, which defined or reduced them to precision
- numbering them to express their mathematical magnitude (precise amount)
- indicating their position (or number) in a group or in a series or as a mark of identification (as a physical faculty may be given the number one because it was made first, and another may be given the number two because it was made second, and so on)
- giving them forms or particular disposition, which distinguished their mien from that of every other physical faculty

- designating their boundaries (limiting their extent)
- fitting their endowments (as the character of physical faculties is to be mutable, to change, and to be altered in form, qualities, or nature)
- qualifying them to exercise their function, and
- adapting them to suit the demands of the physical body and influences from the soul

Hence, the extent of the physical faculties encompassed figuring, defining, forming ideas, images, or models of the faculty Ænosh—and afterward particularizing them. That is to say, the models of the physical faculties of corporeal man were given definite continuance of being and individuality (separate, or distinct existence). However, they had not reached their point of perfection, for they were in their embryonic state, tending in the direction in which or toward which the desire of the universal mind worked or moved. Further, *shemoneh* reveals that the physical faculties grew to a great size and were free and unencumbered to develop to the extent of Ænôsh's circumscription and the desire of the universal mind to manifest them exteriorly.

Mæôth reveals that their development was a sympathetic movement and a reciprocal action in harmony and accord with divine laws, and it was a transition, which—according to the meaning of the Hebrew word *shanah*—caused the universal mind to mutate universally and ontologically, connoting changes in the nature, essence, qualities, and attributes of the universal mind. These changes brought diversity and variations of the physical faculties relative to the diverse mutations of the universal mind.

MANIFESTATION OF PHYSICAL FACULTIES

The Hebrew words *iôled banîm w-banôth* ascertains their diversity. The universal mind emanated many male/female physical faculties resembling Ænôsh. They characterized Ænosh's circumscriptive extent and defined Ænosh's external forms or inclosing of its boundaries. They were the selfsameness of Ænosh and were to be endowed to the souls of men for the purpose of bringing to the circumference (the material world) the strengths, weaknesses, virtues, and vices of corporeal man. Moreover, they were designed to bring to pass the instabilities, caducities, and infirmities of temporal man, all of which the souls must experience in order to evolve with enhanced powers and virtues, realizing the ideal from which they emanated.

SUMMARY

Genesis 5:10 reveals that the universal mind brought forth the physical faculties of corporeal man. The universal mind utilized its invading force (Kainan) as a medium to attain their material existence in matter that was not yet formed.

The underlying meaning of the number 815 was employed by Moses to veil the intricacies of steps taken by the universal mind to produce the physical faculties in material substance.

★ *PRACTICAL APPLICATION*

Genesis 5:10 reveals that developing the physical faculties of corporeal man in material substance conformed to universal harmony and was restricted to regulations according to divine laws. Further, it reveals that these laws possess in them a movement of progression and renewal, which reestablishes, transforms, and regenerates. This tells us that these laws regulate our physical faculties and therefore have an effect on us as we pass from one state to another, developing from childhood to adulthood and into maturity.

Our bodies are always in a state of renewal, reestablishing, transforming, and regenerating. For instance, we can witness the intelligence of the human body in the way an open wound heals within a few days after an injury. Though intangible, we see the effect of divine laws renewing and reestablishing functionality to the injured body part. We can also witness how a child transforms into an adult and how an adult transforms as he reaches maturity.

The cells of our bodies wear out; they come to the end of their usefulness every few minutes and are replaced by new ones, though at a much slower pace as we reach maturity. Our hair changes, the nails grow, the brain cells are alternately charged and recharged. Mental and emotional processes change with the time of day. The weakness of mind experienced in one moment can be transformed into confidence, intellectual force, and moral courage in the next. Wavering and vacillating thoughts can be transformed into steadiness and firmness of mind.

Renewal processes then, are regulated internally by principles fitted in man. One of these principles is the female principle of all generation, which serves as an instrument to form, transform and regenerate man. This female principle fills all of the earthly places and keeps us vitally attuned with its regenerative and transforming power. (Refer to the female principle in chapter 2).

CRITICAL THINKING

1. Genesis 5:10 reveals that the universal mind brought forth the physical faculties of corporeal man. What was the beginning step in this endeavor?
2. Centralization of elements demanded effort, care, and fatigue. What is this statement conveying?
3. The universal mind exerted effort to compress, stabilize, and confine elements from free movement. This was done for what purpose?
4. Centralization of elements brought reconciliation of the seemingly antagonistic forces surrounding the elements. Name the forces.
5. Centralization of elements rendered the spiritual emanation of physical faculties manifest and obvious. What was the first step in attaining their material existence in matter that was not yet form?
6. Even though the physical faculties had been individualized, they had not, according to the underlying meaning of the number eight, reached their point of perfection. This indicates that they were in their _____ _____.

(Answers in Appendix B)

---

1. *Centripetal force* causes objects to follow a circular path. It is a force that is "center-seeking" or "moving toward the center." Gravitational and electrical forces can be transmitted across empty space to produce centripetal forces. The moon, for example, is held in an almost circular orbit by gravitational force directed toward the center of the earth. The orbiting electrons in atoms

experience an electrical force toward the central nuclei (Paul G. Hewitt, *Conceptual Physics*, 122).

2. *Centrifugal force* is an outward force attributed to circular motion and is a result of rotation. It is a force that is "center-fleeing" or "moving away from the center." Centrifugal force effect is attributed not to any real force but to inertia—the tendency of a moving object to follow a straight-line path. Centrifugal force acts on whatever supplies a centripetal force. It is a reaction to centripetal force (ibid., 123–24, 131).

3. The term *quaternary* refers to the four planes (elements) of manifestation of life, which is composed of the buddhic (fire), mental (air), astral (water), and physical (earth) planes (GAG, 605). Scientific studies via satellites reveal that earth, fire, wind, and water join together to create the dynamic environments that shape life in all its forms. Their interaction contributes in creating the environments and the diversity of life we see on earth today ("Earth from Space," *Nova*).

11

PHYSICAL FACULTIES OF CORPOREAL MAN: ÆNOSH'S SIMILITUDES, PART 2

GENESIS 5:11

- Translation from the King James Version of the Bible: "And all the days of Enos were nine hundred and five years and he died."
- The literal English translation as it appears in *The Hebraic Tongue Restored*: "And they were all the days (manifested lights) of Ænosh, five revolving changes, and nine hundreds of revolution: and he deceased."
- Transliteration from *The Hebraic Tongue Restored*: "Wa-îhîou chol-îmeî Ænôsh hamesh shanîm w-theshah mæôth shanah; Wa-îamoth."

The following interpretation of Genesis 5:11 is spiritual in nature, not physical.

PROEM

In the previous chapter, we learned that the physical faculties of corporeal man were brought forth. This chapter reviews and elaborates on their development. The successive transmutation that occurred in the universal mind is also conveyed. Let us begin by examining the events antecedent to the transmutation:

PHYSICAL FACULTIES GETTING AGREEABLE FORMS

The Hebrew words *îhîou chol-îmeî Ænôsh* in Genesis 5:11 make known that the physical faculties of corporeal man (Ænôsh) were arranged, prepared, and given agreeable forms during their luminous period of manifestation. This required advancing (accelerating) all movements of the universally manifesting creative waters to manifest the necessary elements to build the physical faculties. The underlying meaning of the number 905 given in this verse sums up the advent of these faculties and conveys their progression into a consolidated state.

UNDERLYING MEANING OF THE NUMBER 905

To develop the underlying meaning of the number 905, we will examine individually the Hebrew names that make up this number: *hamesh*, *theshah*, and *mæôth*.

Hamesh (number five) discloses how the universal mind made the depths of elementary existence render elements manifest and obvious and how these elements began to be fashioned. It reveals that:

- the universal mind used contractile movements to stir the tumultuous concourse of waters to make the elements palpable and compact (that is, closely and firmly united, as the particles of solid bodies), and subsequently drawn from the depth of their elementary existence.
- being in contact with the elements activated the passive and conditional casuality of the universal mind. It enabled it to

receive impressions, which served to influence how to fashion the physical faculties.

- the plastic power of the universal mind was employed to fashion the elements according to the impressions received.

Shanîm and *theshah* (number nine) convey that the evolving physical faculties underwent mutations as they passed from one state of development to another effecting changes in their boundaries, their designations (which distinguished them from each other), their dispositions or manner in which their parts were arranged, and in their measures, which ascertained their dimensions and reduced them to precision. As a result, the physical faculties were transformed, a gradual process that consolidated their constituent parts, which preserved them from loss and kept them in an entire state.

Their consolidation proceeded by degrees. It cemented, guaranteed, and plastered the faculties. It denotes that the universal mind molded and carefully closed their animated matter. Their animation connotes the physical faculties were quickened, a sequential event after their consolidation. The animated physical faculties were true representatives of Ænosh, qualified to fulfill their nature.

In succession, the universal mind passed from one state of being to another. This was a transitional movement of the universal mind leading to its transmutation and not to the death of Ænosh as translated by the Bible scholars. *Mæôth* ascertains this knowledge.

TRANSMUTATION OF THE UNIVERSAL MIND

The passing from one state of being to another is validated by the Hebrew words *shanah* and *îamoth*. *Shanah* conveys that the universal mind transmuted in cyclic revolutions that encircled this passed period of activities. Once ended, the universal mind returned to its state of seity from whence it had begun to move. *Shanah* discloses that the universal mind was not found at the end of this period of activity in the same state that it was as when it emanated Ænôsh.

Îamoth reveals that the universal mind transformed into a different way of being—the result of having increased its powers from having brought forth Kainan, the medium through which all particular manifestations of the soul may attain material existence, and from having developed the similitudes of Ænôsh thereby given the souls the ability to take to the circumference (the material world) the physical faculties of corporeal man—the contradictory ideas of "being and nothingness," of "strengths and weaknesses," of "virtues and vices"—and its instabilities, caducities, and infirmities, all of which were designed to gradually bring the souls to a greater degree of unfoldment while transiting the physical world. This is the ascension process, the treading of the path, and the steady onward march of consciousness toward the divine.

SUMMARY

Genesis 5:11 reveals how elementary existence rendered the elements necessary to make the physical faculties of corporeal man, how these elements were developed into the physical faculties, and how the physical faculties were quickened. Further, it reveals how the transmutation of the universal mind ensued after ending this period of activities.

★ PRACTICAL APPLICATION

Genesis 5:11 conveys the idea that to bring man to a greater degree of unfoldment, he must experience firsthand all of his physical faculties, instabilities, caducities, and infirmities. This indicates that all the experiences we have had, presently have, and will have are necessary to ascend to realms on high. This concept brings understanding to the many negative and positive conditions we live in. The murderer in one incarnation may be a saint in another; a powerful man in one incarnation may be a weakling in another.

All this is to say that we walk the streets of many lives as pilgrims—until eventually, after many experiences (or many incarnations), the inherent evolutionary impulse moves our unfolding life and the conscious life centers into another and higher class in the great school of life. We begin to tread the path of swift unfoldment and become a willing collaborator with the Cosmic. We obey its laws, follow its designs in detail, and manifest harmonious conditions unmarred by evidences of carelessness or haste. Our steady onward march of consciousness continues, despite the fall, death, and disintegration of our bodies. That is to say, life is indestructible. Therefore, consciousness resulting from the manifestation of life in the physical body unfolds and ascends throughout the periods of manifestations or incarnations.

CRITICAL THINKING

1. Why are the universally manifesting creative waters important to the universal mind?
2. Genesis 5:11 discloses that the elements composing the physical faculties mutated after the universal mind began to fashion them. How did mutation affect the physical faculties?
3. What did the universal mind accomplish during the period of activity before its transformation?

(Answers in Appendix B)

12

MIGHT AND BRIGHTNESS FACULTY OF THE UNIVERSAL MIND: MAHOLALÆL

GENESIS 5:12

- Translation from the King James Version of the Bible: "And Cainan lived seventy years, and begat Mahalale-el."
- The literal English translation as it appears in *The Hebraic Tongue Restored*: "And he lived, Kainan, seven tens of revolving change; and begat the selfsameness of Maholalæl (mighty rising up, brightness)."
- Transliteration from *The Hebraic Tongue Restored*: "Wa-îhî Keînan shibehîm shanah, wa-iôled æth-Maholalæl."

The following interpretation of Genesis 5:12 is spiritual in nature, not physical.

PROEM

We learned in chapter 9 that the faculty Kainan is the invading force of the universal mind, and that Kainan enabled the universal mind to provide the means to attain the material existence of all particular manifestations of the soul in matter that is not yet formed. Now, in this chapter, we are told that possessing this faculty makes it possible for the

96

universal mind to emanate another faculty, *Maholalæl*, a mighty force that aggrandizes "being" and serves as an instrument of generative power to manifest splendor, exaltation, mental elevation, and glory.

MOLDING THE NEW FACULTY

The Hebrew word *îhî* in Genesis 5:12 reveals that elements (protons, electrons, and other constituent ingredients) were manifested and made obvious in response to the universal mind's impulsions upon elementary existence. The Hebrew text discloses that the manifestation of these elements enabled the universal mind to become conscious of its invading force and compressive power (Kainan) being employed to form the new faculty from the elements (unformed matter). The elements were suitable to be put into action, to produce, particularize, or individualize the new faculty. To illustrate, it is likened to molding pottery with moist clay. The hands of the artist (the means) begin to fashion the clay (unformed matter) into a pot (the new faculty). This individualization of unformed matter is explained in the underlying meaning of the number seventy given in this verse.

UNDERLYING MEANING OF THE NUMBER 70

To extract the meaning of the number seventy, its Hebrew name *shibehîm* was divided into its simplest components (*shi-shb-b-be-eh-bho-hi-im*) and subsequently examined.

The underlying meaning of *shibehîm* reveals that the individualization of unformed matter renders real and evident existences (faculties). Though perceived by the universal mind, the new faculty had not yet reached its point of departure (had not yet begun to be formed), nor was it ready for its growth or material development.

Perceiving the new faculty was the result of an interior and active action within the abyss of the unlimited, negative, feminine potentiality of the universal mind. Its female principle was stimulated to generate or bring forth its conception. The stimulation was violent in nature (like a sudden irruption), precipitated, harsh, and inordinate. It was an impelling force that pricked, spurred, roused, or incited the universal mind to greater activity, subsequently manifesting its mental conception in growth and material development—that is, in an external appearance whose accumulated mass manifested universally. The advent of this new faculty became apparent as repeated mutations of the universal mind ensued.

A NEW FACULTY IS BORN

The Hebrew word *shanah* reveals that the universal mind underwent universal and ontological mutations, which caused changes in the nature, essence, qualities, and attributes of the universal mind; it altered the universal mind in form, marking the coming of its new faculty, *Maholalæl*.

MAHOLALÆL

Maholalæl is the rising might and brightness faculty of the universal mind. The Hebrew text discloses that this faculty enables the universal mind to endow the souls of men with a strong potential for exaltation, greatness, dignity, splendor, and glory. With this new emanation, the universal mind brought forth a very strong or vigorous faculty, powerful in every way—physically, mentally, morally, or spiritually.

Maholalæl:

- refines or subtilizes man's qualities and virtues;

- brings great bodily strength or physical power to the faculties of corporeal man;
- tends to aggrandize and exalt *being*, in power, rank, or honor;
- tends to the entire development of *being*;
- serves as an instrument of generative power to manifest exteriorly the power of *being* and that which extends, rises, unfolds, makes resplendent, elevates, and glorifies *being*;
- is an exalting and glorifying movement without end. Its duration is limitless;
- attains the desired end: to aggrandize and develop *being*;
- recovers (makes good again) and arrives in or conducts to safety (preserves *being*); and
- emits an eccentric force that tends toward the aggrandizement of *being*.

ADAM'S MICROCOSM (5/10)

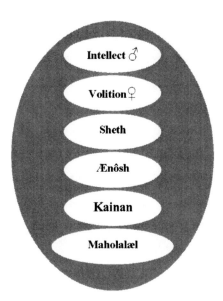

Figure 12.1 above shows the faculties of Adam within his microcosm are now composed of intellect (male principle); volition/will (female

principle); Sheth (Adam's power to frame the foundation of the soul); Ænosh (Adam's physical faculties, corporeal man); Kainan (Adam's general invading force); and Maholalæl (Adam's might and brightness).

SUMMARY

Genesis 5:12 reveals that the universal mind became conscious of its invading and compressive power being employed as a means to form a new faculty. It reveals that mutations enabled the universal mind to bring forth the new faculty and that this faculty gives the souls of men a strong potential for exaltation, greatness, dignity, splendor, and glory.

★ PRACTICAL APPLICATION

Genesis 5:12 reveals that man has been given the power for greatness, splendor, and glory, but few know they have that capacity. Ancient philosophy reveals that humanity, through the ages, has witnessed the majority of people living in a state of want. They are not able to think beyond their immediate needs, and they tend to follow the great man and woman who excel. Some may say that there are leaders and followers and that not everyone can lead because we have different levels of consciousness in this world.

It is true that there are different levels of consciousness in humanity, but all beings have "visions that they glorify in their mind. They are ideals that they enthrone in their hearts" (James Allen, *As a Man Thinketh*). But most beings are not aware that they can build their lives upon these ideals and *become*. How then can the majority of people be taught that they too can lead, that they too can aggrandize and exalt their being in power, rank, or honor? The answer is simple: they can be taught through education or cultivation and training of the mind, through the acquisition or imparting of knowledge.

CRITICAL THINKING

1. Genesis 5:12 reveals that a new faculty was brought forth by the universal mind. What is the name of this faculty?
2. For what purpose was this faculty created?
3. What was the beginning step to bring forth this faculty?
4. Where was the conception of this new faculty perceived?
5. What is required to make the conception of the universal mind a reality?
6. What incites the universal mind to greater activity?

(Answers in Appendix B)

13

MEDIUMS OF CONSCIOUSNESS FOR THE SOULS OF MEN: KAINAN'S SIMILITUDES, PART 1

GENESIS 5:13

- Translation from the King James Version of the Bible: "And Cainan lived after he begat Mahalaleel eight hundred and forty years and begat sons and daughters."
- The literal English translation as it appears in *The Hebraic Tongue Restored*: "And he lived, Kainan, after the causing him to beget that same Mahollæl, four tens of revolving change, and eight hundreds of revolution and he begat sons and daughters (many issued offspring)."
- Transliteration from *The Hebraic Tongue Restored*: "Wa îhî Keînan âhoreî hôlid-o æth-Maholalæl ârbahîm shanah w-shemoneh mæôth shanah w-iôled banîm w-banôth."

The following interpretation of Genesis 5:13 is spiritual in nature, not physical.

PROEM

In chapter 9 we were informed that the universal mind developed Kainan, a faculty that serves as a medium through which anything can be done or carried out. In this chapter, this medium is brought to our awareness again. Kainan will serve as a prototype from which *similitudes* or *mediums* will be made as an evolutionary process of making man.

Genesis 5:13 addresses the production of these mediums or means through which all particular manifestations of individual being can be attained. These mediums will be the means of transmission of mental, emotional, astral, and physical consciousness, that by or through them the continuance of being can be manifested in the material world.

Further, Genesis 5:13 relates to us how the universal mind centralized elements (electrons, protons, and other constituent ingredients) to produce the mediums. These are the so-called sons and daughters of Cainan mentioned in the Holy Bible. In other words, the sons and daughters of Cainan are the agglomerated mediums that resulted from the centralization of these elements.

At this point, it would be well to mention (as a matter of importance) the *etheric double*,[1] the perfect duplicate and finer counterpart of the physical body. Like mediums, the *etheric double* also transmits, but its transmission is that of *archæus* or *vital life force* (synonymous with the astral light or spiritual air of the ancients) to the physical form. Its main function is to absorb vitality and distribute it to the physical body and to act as an intermediary between its dense counterpart (the physical body) and the astral body. It transmits the consciousness of physical sense contact through the etheric brain to the astral body, and it also transmits the consciousness from the astral, emotional, and mental bodies down into the physical brain and nervous system.

The *etheric double* is not able to act as a separate vehicle of consciousness in which man can live or function as when he lives or functions in his mental, emotional, astral, and physical mediums. The diffuse consciousness of the etheric double belongs to the physical form, has no mentality, and does not readily serve as a medium of mentality when separated from its dense counterpart. Paracelsus[2] (a great physician of the Middle Ages) called this vehicle or etheric double *Mumia*.

Mumias can be physical or spiritual. For instance, vaccines are considered physical mumias, in that they are the vehicles of a semi-astral virus. Other examples are nerves, which are conduits of sensation, and blood vessels, which are conduits of blood. Modern science has accepted *ether* as the most universal form of Mumia intervening between the realms of vital energy and of organic and inorganic substance. Whether organic or inorganic, physical or spiritual, anything used to transmit the archæus is termed a Mumia.

The notion gained by observing the difference between mediums and etheric doubles will remove any misconceptions as to their distinct functions. Mediums are vehicles of consciousness, the organized bodies on different planes of existence in which souls abide and express themselves. Etheric doubles are, to a small extent, vehicles of transmission, but they have no consciousness on their own.

Let us now return to the making and development of Kainan's similitudes: the mediums.

GENERATING MEDIUMS FOR THE CONTINUANCE OF BEING

The Hebrew word *îhî* in Genesis 5:13 reveals that the elements to build mediums were manifested and made obvious in response to the universal mind's impulsions upon elementary existence. *Îhî* discloses that these elements were readily perceived and apprehended by the universal mind. Their apprehension enabled the universal mind to become conscious of certain properties and states pertaining to its compressive and agglomerative power (Kainan) providing the means to mold the elements into mediums.

The Hebrew word *âhoreî* given in this verse reveals that:

- Compacting or centralizing the elements was the beginning step of molding the mediums.
- The act of centralizing served to identify the accumulated elements as being the ones to produce the intended effect.
- This centralizing movement united and reconciled the seeming contrarieties or antagonistic forces (centripetal and centrifugal forces[3]) surrounding the elements.
- Because centralization drew the elements to a central point, it rendered their identity manifest and obvious.

RECONCILIATION OF ANTAGONISTIC FORCES

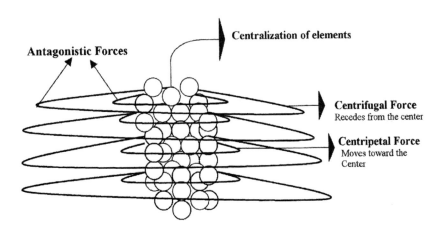

Figure 13.1 above depicts the centralization of elements taking place at the reconciliation of two opposing forces, one tending to recede from the center (centrifugal), and the other tending to move toward the center (centripetal).

Âhoreî relates that the accumulated elements resulted in an effluvium, or ethereal, spirituous emanations, an invisible form of the mediums that represented their potential life or power of being.

The Hebrew word *hôlid* reveals that their power to exist resulted from binding their nonbeing (nonexistence) to being—that is, from the universal mind passing the effluvium from one nature to another in an eccentric movement designed to extend, rise, and unfold the effluvium in all directions within its sphere of activity. This eccentric movement affected the universal mind. It expanded its intellectual powers, enabling it to understand how to progressively build the mediums.

By laying the effluvium open for view and contemplation, it made known the procedure that showed the universal mind how to seize and unite electrons, protons, and other constituent ingredients to form atoms and subsequently create coalitions that would unite the atoms into a mass.

Coalitions led the universal mind to link the atoms in successive series and to maintain them fixed and in union with a degree of density or spissitude (not perfectly liquid nor perfectly solid) that bound them by natural attraction, as the constituent particles of homogeneous bodies unite in a mass and tend toward each other, bonding universally. In succession, the universal mind executed its power of acting and dominion over the universal quaternary[4] and over its faculty Maholalæl enabling it to aggrandize the progressive movement of the atomic mass. The underlying meaning of the number 840 given in this verse unveils the details.

UNDERLYING MEANING OF THE NUMBER 840

To accurately unveil the meaning of the number 840 requires that the three Hebrew names composing this number—*ârbahîm*, *shemoneh*, and *mæôth*—be examined individually.

Ârbahîm (number forty) reveals that the universal mind aggrandized the atomic mass in a direct, vigorous, and productive rectilinear movement that multiplied endlessly the mass numerical extent.

The rectilinear movement tended toward augmenting and propagating the atomic mass. It was a large and broad movement that increased the mass in volume and is expressed by the adverbial relations "much," "more," "still more," and "many." It is likened to "atoms combining to form molecules, in turn combining to form compounds and substances of matter" similar to "atoms increasing in volume as they combine to become solids, liquids, gases, and plasma."[5]

The broad movement encompassed all ideas of multitude, number, quantity, the strength or power drawn from numbers, and the action of being carried in a mass. Hieroglyphically, it is the four-fold power or quaternary involving in matter every idea of strength, solidity, and greatness, resulting from the extent and numerical multiplication of the atomic mass.

Ârbahîm reveals that the rectilinear movement began as an interior and active action within the universal mind. It expresses a sort of movement by which the universal mind was instrumental in developing all ideas of progression, of gradual going (involuting the atomic mass into matter), and of advancing the qualities or attributes of the developing mediums.

Involuting the atomic mass into matter was a precipitated, harsh, inordinate movement made by the universal mind to drive the attributes of the evolving mediums into matter in order to manifest their growth and material development. This movement was a goad, or an impelling force (the female principle) within the universal mind that incited it to manifest the mediums universally.

The Hebrew word *shanah* reveals that the universal mind underwent repeated mutations as it passed from one state to another endeavoring to develop the mediums into precise forms. Subsequently, the universal mind rendered images, representations, or similitudes of its faculty Kainan (the mediums) in material substance.

Shemoneh (number eight) reveals that the mediums circumscribed the extent of Kainan. This means that all particulars and detailed accounts of Kainan's attributes were endowed to the mediums. That is to say, the mediums had the general invading force, the compressive and decisive power and the agglomerative or repressive force of Kainan, and they were to serve as vehicles of consciousness to individualize the existence proper of souls in the mental, emotional, astral, and physical planes of existence. This required to classify the mediums by type: corresponding to the souls of men, as opposed to any other soul life (animals); to sort them by gender: male and female mediums; to place them in the highest division of soul life: mankind's; and to classify them as resembling Kainan collectively, as opposed to any other faculty of the universal mind (Sheth, Ænosh).

The extent of the mediums encompassed:

- describing them by their properties or peculiar qualities (mental, emotional, astral, physical);
- obtaining their proper measure, which ascertained the dimensions that defined or reduced them to precision;
- assigning their number(s) to express their mathematical magnitude or precise amount (as in counting), to indicate their position (or number) in a group or in a series of

particular productions, and to count the number of mediums in a plurality, as expressing their total;

- giving them forms;
- establishing their determination, boundaries, or limits to their extent;
- stipulating all qualifications that they may exercise their function; and
- endowing them with the ability to adapt to the demands of each individual soul.

Circumscribing the extent of the mediums means that they were particularized; they were given a definite distinct existence or individuality, though embryonic in state. At this stage of development, they had not yet reached their point of perfection, for they were still evolving.

Mæôth confirms that the mediums were made to develop to the extent of Kainan's circumscription and the desire of the universal mind to manifest them exteriorly. These were transitional movements that led the universal mind to mutate repeatedly and consequently manifested changes in its nature, essence, qualities, and attributes. They altered the universal mind in form enabling it to bring forth the mediums in the order of things, or in the order of time relative to its diverse mutations. *Shanah* concurs with this knowledge.

EMANATING THE MEDIUMS OF CONSCIOUSNESS

The Hebrew words *iôled banîm w-banôth* validate the universal mind emanated a great multitude of mediums resembling its faculty Kainan. They characterized Kainan's circumscriptive extent and the definition of Kainan's inclosing boundaries. They were Kainan's sameness, providing the means through which all particular manifestations of the souls can be attained.

SUMMARY

Genesis 5:13 reveals that *mediums of consciousness* or means through which all particular manifestations of the souls can be attained were brought forth. Further, it reveals that these *mediums* are means of transmission; by them or through them, the continuance of being can be manifested in the material world. This verse also relates the process that took place in making the mediums, which was concealed under the number 840.

★ PRACTICAL APPLICATION

In this chapter we learned the functions of the *etheric double*, the finer counterpart of man. We learned that the *etheric double* is a vehicle for the *archæus* (vital life force), which Paracelsus called *Mumia.* It is of interest to note that Paracelsus believed that the cause of much disease was the derangement of this Mumia. He thought that the Mumia, being much finer in its substances than the earthly body, was far more susceptible to impulses and inharmonies, and that a person with a morbid mental attitude could poison his own etheric nature (his Mumia). This infection, diverting the natural flow of vital life force, would later appear as a physical ailment. He advocated the idea that preventing physical ailments as a result of morbid thinking necessitates controlling the vital life force or archæus.

But controlling the archæus is virtually impossible, save through one of its vehicles (the Mumia). Food is a good example of this. We secure nourishment when we incorporate their structures into our own body by eating them. This means that we gain control over the Mumia, or the etheric double, of the animal or plant. Obtaining this control diverts the flow of the vital life force to its own uses. According to Paracelsus, "that which constitutes life is contained in the Mumia, and by imparting the Mumia we impart life" (Manly P. Hall, *The Secret Teachings of All Ages*).

When we impart the Mumia of certain herbs and flowers we re-harmonize our body with the vital energy that is in them. According to hermetic herbalism, this energy supplies the elements needed to overcome physical ailments. "When properly taken, herbs and flowers could be used for the alleviation of suffering, or for the development of spiritual, mental, moral, or physical powers" (Ibid.) Herbs and flowers help man regain control of the archæus. This results in healing his etheric nature previously poisoned by morbid mental attitudes.

CRITICAL THINKING

1. Genesis 5:13 addresses the production of mediums through which all particular manifestations of individual being can be attained. What are mediums within the context of this verse?

2. The *etheric double* was discussed in this chapter. What name did Paracelsus give to the etheric double?

3. Mumias can be both physical and spiritual. Give three examples of physical Mumias and their function.

4. The most universal form of Mumia is ether. It is a substance intervening between the realm of _____ _____ and that of _____ and _____ substance.

---

5. What is the relationship between mediums of consciousness and the faculty Kainan?

6. Compacting or centralizing elements was the beginning step of molding the mediums of consciousness. What was the purpose of centralizing these elements?

7. Elements were formed into atoms and subsequently into an atomic mass. Number forty (part of the number 840 given in Genesis 5:13) discloses a productive rectilinear movement, which augmented and propagated the atomic mass. How is this increased in volume adverbially expressed?

8. Number forty encompasses all ideas of multitude, number, quantity, and the strength or power drawn from _____.

(Answers in Appendix B)

1. The *etheric double*, which diffuses itself throughout the molecules of the human body, is the body's finer counterpart, constituting the vehicle of *archæus* (vital life force), and may be called a *vital body*. This *etheric appendage* is not dissipated by death but remains until the physical form is completely decomposed. Belief in the so-called ghosts seen around graveyards is nothing more than etheric doubles awaiting full decomposition of their denser counterpart.

2. Paracelsus was a great physician of the Middle Ages, also known as the "Second Hermes" and the "Trismegistus of Switzerland." He "devoted his entire life to the study and exposition of Hermetic philosophy," and he is "yet to be recognized as the greatest physician of all times." Paracelsus "was one of the few minds who intelligently sought to reconcile the art of healing with the philosophic and religious systems of paganism and Christianity." His real

name was Theophrastus of Hohenheim (Manly P. Hall, *The Secret Teachings of All Ages*, 109).

3. Centripetal and centrifugal forces: refer to footnotes 1 and 2 in chapter 10.

4. *Quaternary*: refer to the footnote 3 in chapter 10.

5. Paul G. Hewitt, *Conceptual Physics*.

14

MEDIUMS OF CONSCIOUSNESS FOR THE SOULS OF MEN: KAINAN'S SIMILITUDES, PART 2

GENESIS 5:14

- Translation from the King James Version of the Bible: "And all the days of Cainan were nine hundred and ten years: and he died."
- The literal English translation as it appears in *The Hebraic Tongue Restored*: "And they were, all the days (manifested lights) of Kainan, ten revolving changes, and nine hundreds of revolution; and he deceased."
- Transliteration from *The Hebraic Tongue Restored*: "Wa-îhîou chol-îmeî Keînan hesher shanîm w-theshah mæoth shanah: wa-îamôth."

The following interpretation of Genesis 5:14 is spiritual in nature, not physical.

PROEM

We learned in chapter 13 that similitudes of the faculty Kainan were produced and that these were a great multitude of mediums—means through which all particular manifestations of individual being could be attained in the material world. In succession, Genesis 5:14 relates to us the progression of these mediums and the transmutation of the universal mind, which followed.

ADVANCING THE MEDIUMS OF CONSCIOUSNESS

The Hebrew words *îhîou chol îmeî Keînan* in Genesis 5:14 give an overview of what took place in producing the mediums of consciousness.

1. The mediums of consciousness were arranged, prepared, and given agreeable forms during their luminous period of manifestation.
2. It involved accelerating all movements of the creative waters to render the necessary elements to build the mediums.
3. The faculty Kainan was the blue print from which the mediums were modeled.

Advancing the mediums into material substance required the aggregative and reforming power of the universal mind. The following interpretation of the number 910 given in this verse unveils this activity.

UNDERLYING MEANING OF THE NUMBER 910

Number 910 discloses the progression of the mediums as they were driven into denser forms. We will scrutinize the Hebrew names composing this number—*hesher, theshah,* and *mæoth*—to render the particulars.

Hesher (number ten) makes known that the aggregative and reforming power (formative energy) of the universal mind formed the mediums, and that its congregation of power proper, of elementary motive force that governs every motive principle—or that which incites to action or causes motion—directed their evolution downward toward the lower planes of existence. It conveys that the universal mind guided and regulated the mediums as they were driven toward the material, low-down, and degraded sentient existence.

The force needed to drive the mediums toward physical reality had to be so powerful (as the number ten) in order to thrust the mediums to their densest form: their envelopment into material substance corresponding to their nature—whether mental, emotional, astral, or physical.

Hesher reveals that the mediums were a tumultuous concourse, strong and vigorous, which the universal mind directed according to just, luminous laws modeled upon the immutable laws of order and universal harmony.

QUICKENING THE MEDIUMS OF CONSCIOUSNESS

The Hebrew word *shanîm* reveals that the mediums underwent mutation as they were driven into material substance. But, nothing passes from one state to another without passing through all its intermediate states. This is the Law of Continuity and Reciprocity. *Theshah* (number nine) reveals that the mediums were influenced as they were impelled into denser forms. Gradually, the universal mind cemented (joined closely), guaranteed, and plastered the mediums. Their boundaries, designations, definitions, and measures were transformed. It made their constituent parts denser, which preserved them from loss, and kept them in an entire state. By degrees the universal mind gradually shaped and carefully closed the mediums' animated matter, which quickened them following the consolidating actions of the universal mind. This marks the ending of a period of activity and a transition for the universal mind followed. *Mæôth* concurs with this knowledge.

TRANSMUTATION OF THE UNIVERSAL MIND

The Hebrew word *shanah* reveals that the transmutation was cyclic in nature. The successive changes revolved around this beginning and ending period of activities. Upon ending, the universal mind returned to its state of seity, the state from whence it had begun to move. Further, it reveals that the universal mind was not found at the end of this period of activities in the same state that it was as when it emanated Kainan.

The Hebrew word *iamoth* discloses that the universal mind had transformed to a different way of being denoting that it had grown in stature: first, from having brought forth its "might and brightness" faculty, Maholalæl, a very strong and vigorous faculty whose purpose is to tend to the entire aggrandizement of being, and second, from having developed its ability to produce the similitudes of Kainan, the directing force that serves to manifest all particular manifestations of the soul—that is, all minuteness of details, all separate or distinct existences, and all endowments of qualities.

Under the Law of Cause and Effect, Kainan served as an efficient cause. It impelled the universal mind to act on its plans to individualize the existence proper of souls, thereby advancing their continuance of being toward the material. That is to say, possessing the faculty Kainan enabled the universal mind to distinguish the peculiar properties (qualities) of the mediums and bring them forth—the mediums being the various vestures of the souls (mental, emotional, astral, and physical vehicles of consciousness). These mediums of consciousness wrap the souls as they continue their descent toward the material.

SOUL INVOLVING INTO MEDIUMS OF CONSCIOUSNESS AS IT DESCENDS INTO THE MATERIAL WORLD

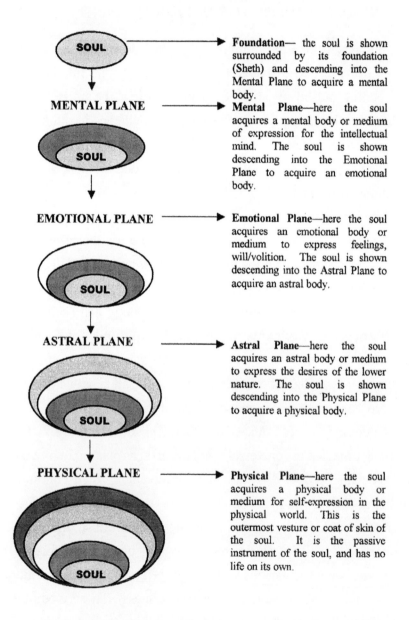

SOUL

Foundation— the soul is shown surrounded by its foundation (Sheth) and descending into the Mental Plane to acquire a mental body.

MENTAL PLANE

SOUL

Mental Plane—here the soul acquires a mental body or medium of expression for the intellectual mind. The soul is shown descending into the Emotional Plane to acquire an emotional body.

EMOTIONAL PLANE

SOUL

Emotional Plane—here the soul acquires an emotional body or medium to express feelings, will/volition. The soul is shown descending into the Astral Plane to acquire an astral body.

ASTRAL PLANE

SOUL

Astral Plane—here the soul acquires an astral body or medium to express the desires of the lower nature. The soul is shown descending into the Physical Plane to acquire a physical body.

PHYSICAL PLANE

SOUL

Physical Plane—here the soul acquires a physical body or medium for self-expression in the physical world. This is the outermost vesture or coat of skin of the soul. It is the passive instrument of the soul, and has no life on its own.

SUMMARY

In this chapter, Genesis 5:14 reveals that the aggregative and reforming power of the universal mind, as well as its congregation of power proper regulated the mediums of consciousness as they were driven toward the material. Further, it reveals that the universal mind transformed into a different way of being after quickening the mediums.

★ PRACTICAL APPLICATION

We learned from the previous chapter that *etheric doubles* are *vehicles of archæus*, or vital life force. It is beneficial to know that the etheric nature of the human body is of extreme tenuity and elasticity, and that it is diffused throughout the molecules of the body for the transmission of light and heat. Light is essential to all living things. Ancient philosophies assert that the light we get from the sun is the source of our vitality or life. It has a direct influence upon consciousness and intelligence—and especially upon the systematic, harmonious regulation of the various conscious and unconscious actions in our body. Sunlight is intended to vitalize our bodies, keep our skin healthy, and cause us to breathe energy.

If the etheric nature of our bodies becomes weakened as a result of morbid mental attitudes, we will not be able to absorb properly the vital qualities contained in the light. These are the colors that are in white sunlight: blue, green, yellow, orange, purple, infrared or bright red. The resulting effect is illness in the physical body. When we are physically weak, it helps us to eat fruits and vegetables. Plant life in the vegetables and fruits we eat are charged with energy by the sun's emanations upon them. "Eating" light buys us time to heal our etheric nature as we endeavor to correct our "stinking thinking."

CRITICAL THINKING

1. What is the underlying meaning of number ten—part of the number 910 given in Genesis 5:14?
2. The force needed to drive the mediums to physical reality had to be very powerful in order to thrust the mediums to their densest form. What power could be so strong as to be capable of doing this?
3. Mutation causes changes. This means that the mediums were _____.
4. Nothing passes from one state to another without passing through all its intermediate states. This is a law. What is the name of this law?
5. The universal mind transformed into a different way of being after effecting the purpose for which its faculty Kainan was emanated. For transmutation to occur a law was in operation. Which law was this?

(Answers in Appendix B)

15

STEADFASTNESS AND PERSEVERANCE: IARED

GENESIS 5:15

- Translation from the King James Version of the Bible: "And Mahalaleel lived sixty and five years, and begat Jared."
- The literal English translation as it appears in *The Hebraic Tongue Restored*: "And he lived, Mahollæl, five revolving changes, and six tens of revolution; and he begat the selfsameness of Ired (the steadfast one)."
- Transliteration from *The Hebraic Tongue Restored*: "Wa îhî Maholalæl hamesh shanîm w-shishîm shanah wa-iôled æth-Iared."

The following interpretation of Genesis 5:15 is spiritual in nature, not physical.

PROEM

It is the beginning of a new period of activity for the universal mind, and another faculty is due to come forth. From Genesis 5:12, recall the faculty Kainan enabled the universal mind to emanate a mighty force (Maholalæl) whose purpose is to aggrandize being. In this verse, we are told that this mighty force enabled the universal mind to emanate another faculty—its "steadfast and persevering" powers. The Hebrew text reveals that these are two aspects of the new faculty.

In steadfastness, the universal mind is fixed and firm; that is, it is firmly fixed or established. It is constant and resolute, not fickle or wavering. In its persevering mode, the universal mind continues on a given course out of a desire to obtain something. It persists from a determination of *will* (its female principle) not to give up. Here, the universal mind is constant in the execution of a purpose or enterprise. *Will* impels the universal mind to act on its conceptions until the desired end is attained.

Genesis 5:15 reveals that this new faculty enables the universal mind to move souls either upward (good) or downward (evil) in a steadfast and persevering mode. The upward movement is the ascension process in evolution, which is accomplished through the soul's own divine life (enhanced with powers and virtues) realizing the ideal from which it emanated. The downward movement is the soul's descent into matter of the lower planes during the process of involution, limiting itself in form and involving in matter all its qualities and potencies. Hence, in this chapter, we will elaborate upon the emanation of *Iared*, the steadfast and persevering faculty of the universal mind, which Maholalæl was instrumental in bringing forth.

THE BUILDING OF A NEW FACULTY

We learned in previous chapters that the Hebrew word *îhî* indicates that the universal mind is acting upon elementary existence to manifest the necessary elements to build conceivable *beings* (faculties and their similitudes). We also learned that the manifestation of these elements enables the universal mind to become conscious of the properties and states that pertain to its faculties.

At this stage of development, the Hebrew text reveals that the universal mind became conscious of its faculty *Maholalæl* serving as an instrument to generate the power needed to build the new faculty. The underlying meaning of the number sixty-five given in this verse reveals the great effort exerted in this endeavor.

UNDERLYING MEANING OF THE NUMBER 65

Hamesh and *shishîm* are the two Hebrew names composing the number sixty-five. Their elucidation was made simple by dividing these names into their simplest components—*h-ha-hou-am-me-msh* and *shi-ish-shsh-im*—and finding their meaning in the radical vocabulary.

Hamesh (number five) reveals that the universal mind exerted great effort upon elementary existence to render elements manifest and obvious. This was a violent effort characterized by the exertion of a rapid force that stirred the passive, creative waters and made the elements palpable and compact, in turn, enabling the universal mind to draw them from their depth.

Upon contacting the elements, the passive and conditional casuality of the universal mind became active. It enabled it to receive impressions that influenced its plastic power or ability to fashion the elements in accordance to the impressions received.

The Hebrew word *shanîm* relates that fashioning the elements caused them to mutate resulting in a real and evident existence that manifested in substance. *Shishîm* (number sixty) discloses that the evolving faculty was substantialized in proportional measures and in like nature as the universal mind, fitted and suitable to be developed universally.

Just as the elements mutated so did the universal mind. *Shanah* reveals that the universal mind underwent universal and ontological mutations. These were momentary changes (consequence of mutations) that lasted only while the universal mind remained in one state, and they changed when the universal mind mutated into another state. With each new state, the universal mind carried with it all the changes from previous mutations. These changes empowered the universal mind to develop its new faculty and to subsequently bring it forth. Moses named it Iared.

IARED

Iared is the steadfast and persevering faculty that gives the universal mind the power to move souls upward or downward. It is the power to be fast, firmly fixed, or established with resoluteness. It is the power to persist in anything undertaken, either upward or downward. Possessing this power enables the universal mind to continue an effect, even after the cause that first gave rise to the effect is removed, similar to the way the impression of light on the eye persists after the luminous object has been withdrawn, or the way motion persists in an object after the moving force is withdrawn.

The natural sense contained by Iared is that of perseverance and steadfastness that follows an imparted or shared movement— either upward (good) or downward (evil). Yes, this movement can be good or evil, ascending or descending, as is proved by the two verbs springing from the name *Iared*: *rod*, which means to govern or dominate, and *irod*, which signifies to sink or descend.

HIEROGLYPHIC MEANING OF THE NAME *IARED*

Hieroglyphically, the Hebrew name *Iared* discloses the manifestation of potential faculties or latent powers that begin as a visible effluvium—a fluidic, ethereal, spirituous emanation—that spreads out, unfolds, occupies space, and takes possession of something by the effect of a steady, indefinite movement of the soul. This is a repeated movement that turns to itself, is propagated circularly, and moves with firmness, either ascending or descending, persevering in its will, the domination that is the natural bent of steadfastness and strength of soul.

The soul ascends in the process of evolution accomplished through its own divine life, supplemented by the love energy responding from above to its aspirations below. It rises with enhanced powers and virtues and realizes the ideal from which it emanated. Or the soul descends into matter of the lower planes during the process of involution, limiting itself in form and involving all its qualities and potencies into matter.

This is the propagated circular movement of the soul (ascending and descending), which perseveres in its will to dominate, rule, govern, predominate over, influence most prominently, have the greatest effect upon, give specific character or appearance to, and overshadow. These characteristics are the natural bent of steadfastness and strength of soul, and they unfold while the soul is enveloped in its protective enclosure or covering—the organical boundary (physical form) in the temporal and sensible sphere, extracted from boundless and foregone time.

DIVINE PURPOSE IN MANIFESTATION

The divine purpose in manifestation is to involve myriad of souls in matter (descent) that they may return again by evolution (ascent) after having accomplished the end for which they involved in matter—namely, for their growth and exaltation. This growth and exaltation of the souls can be accomplished because of Maholalæl, a powerful faculty endowed to each soul to aggrandize its being and to serve as an instrument of generative power to manifest exteriorly splendor, mental elevation, and glory. (Refer to the full meaning of *Maholalæl* in chapter 12.)

ADAM'S MICROCOSM (6/10)

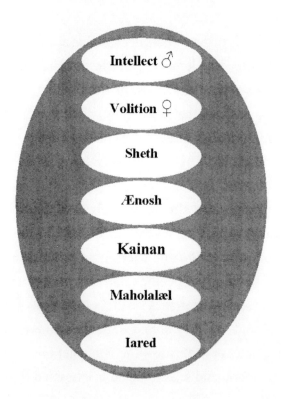

Figure 15.1 above shows the addition of Iared to Adam's microcosm, which is now composed of intellect (male principle), volition/will (female principle), Sheth (Adam's power to frame the foundation of the soul), Ænosh (Adam's physical faculties, corporeal man), Kainan (Adam's general invading force), Maholalæl (Adam's rising might and brightness), and Iared (Adam's power of steadfastness and perseverance).

SUMMARY

Genesis 5:15 reveals the advent of the universal mind's power of steadfastness and perseverance, a shared movement that drives the souls either upward (via evolution) or downward (via involution).

★ PRACTICAL APPLICATION

In this chapter, the advent of the steadfast and persevering faculty of the universal mind is disclosed. We know from chapter 1 that the universal mind is composed of the assemblage of all minds (souls of humanity). As such, our souls are endowed with that steadfast and persevering faculty as well.

We learned that this faculty imparts a shared movement upward (good) or downward (evil). Our soul utilizes this faculty to go up (ascend) through evolution or to go down (descend) and involute into matter. Our souls can also use this faculty to elevate our thoughts (good) or to sink our thinking into the depths of despondency (evil).

We can, for example, recognize the good and the beauty within us by withdrawing into our own soul (the holy place), or we can seek to realize beauty outside ourselves by laborious productions—the constant effort to attract things we think are beautiful in the material world. Instead of going out into the manifold, we can forsake it for our soul, and so float upward toward the divine fount of being, whose stream floats within us.

CRITICAL THINKING

1. Genesis 5:15 reveals that a new faculty was brought forth. What are the powers of this new faculty?

2. Describe steadfastness as portrayed in the context of this book.

3. Describe perseverance as portrayed in the context of this book.

4. Genesis 5:15 reveals that this new faculty enables the universal mind to move souls either upward (good) or downward (evil). Explain what good and evil mean in this context.

5. What is the name of this new faculty?

6. The hieroglyphic interpretation of the name *Iared* discloses that it means the manifestation of potential faculties or latent powers. How are the potential faculties or latent powers begin to manifest?

7. The soul ascends in the process of evolution with enhanced _____ and _____.

8. The soul descends into matter during the process of involution, limiting _____ _____ in _____.

9. Upon descension of the soul, what is being involved in matter?

10. What is the protective enclosure of the soul?

(Answers in Appendix B)

16

MIGHT AND BRIGHTNESS FACULTY FOR THE SOULS OF MEN: MAHOLALÆL'S SIMILITUDES, PART 1

GENESIS 5:16

- Translation from the King James Version of the Bible: "And Mahalaleel lived after he begat Jared eight hundred and thirty years and begat sons and daughters."
- The literal English translation as it appears in *The Hebraic Tongue Restored*: "And he lived, Mahollæl, after the causing him to beget that same Ired, three tens of revolving change and eight hundreds of revolution; And he begat sons and daughters (many issued offspring)."
- Transliteration from *The Hebraic Tongue Restored*: "Wa îhî Maholalæl âhoreî hôlid-ô æth-Iared sheloshîm shanah w-shemoneh mæôth shanah wa-iôled banîm w'banôth."

The following interpretation of Genesis 5:16 is spiritual in nature, not physical.

PROEM

Making similitudes of the faculty Maholalæl is next in this period of activity. Maholalæl will serve as the prototype from which its similitudes (the symbolical sons and daughters of Maholalæl) will be modeled, (1) that through the endowment of this mighty power man may develop his entire being and (2) that through the development of this power he may reach the culminating point of his soul personality (or that which constitutes his lower nature) and become other than what he has been. This carries the notion of a glorified soul, no longer to be entombed within the limitations of the physical body and lower mind. At this stage of development, man can leave his body at will and, without break in consciousness, enter the higher realms of existence—the heaven world.

THE GENERATION OF MAHOLALÆL'S SIMILITUDES

Examination of the Hebrew word *îhî* in Genesis 5:16 reveals that elementary existence was acted upon by the universal mind to render elements (protons, electrons, and other constituent ingredients) manifest and obvious. This caused the universal mind to become conscious of its generative power serving as instrument to generate Maholalæl's similitudes.

The Hebrew word *âhoreî* tells us that all notions attached to Maholalæl's identity were taken into consideration when the elements were compressed, stabilized, and confined from free movement to give them definite forms or expressions that were compacted and centralized, and consequently, to elicit the similitudes' power of being.

Centralization brought reconciliation (stasis) of the antagonistic forces (centripetal and centrifugal forces[1]) surrounding the elements.

Accordingly, it resulted in an effluvium or ethereal spirituous emanations of Maholalæl's similitudes. This conveys that the effluvium (the invisible form of Maholalæl's similitudes) was the manifestation of the similitudes' potential life or power of being. *Hôlid* reveals that their power of being became evident as the effluvium was passed from one nature to another in an eccentric movement directed downward into the sphere of activity where the unfoldment of the effluvium took place. Necessarily, the universal mind acted upon the universal quaternary and its faculty Iared to direct the effluvium downward. This enabled the universal mind to propagate and develop the emanations across the circumference.

The underlying meaning of the number 830 given in this verse elaborates on this downward movement and on the development of the similitudes.

UNDERLYING MEANING OF THE NUMBER 830

The Hebrew names *sheloshîm*, *shemoneh*, and *mœôth* compose the number 830. After dividing each name into their monosyllabic components, the radical vocabulary was used as a guide to unveil their underlying meaning.

Sheloshîm (number thirty) reveals that the universal mind propagated the effluvium in a circular downward movement that spread across the entire sphere of activity. This downward movement progressed on the curved line of the sphere like a downward spiral. It was an eccentric movement of the universal mind that went a great distance, to the furthest point to be reached in the polarization of mind and matter, at the circumferential extent.

DOWNWARD PROPAGATING MOVEMENT
OF THE UNIVERSAL MIND

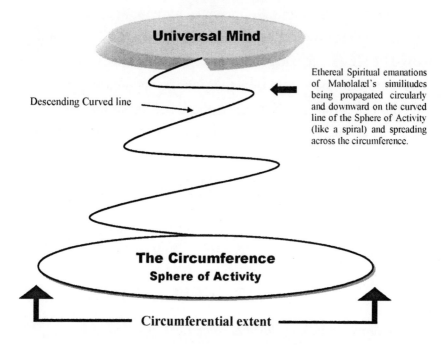

Universal Mind

Descending Curved line

Ethereal Spiritual emanations of Maholalæl's similitudes being propagated circularly and downward on the curved line of the Sphere of Activity (like a spiral) and spreading across the circumference.

The Circumference
Sphere of Activity

Circumferential extent

Figure 16.1 above depicts the eccentric, circular, downward movement of the universal mind and the propagation of the effluvium throughout the circumferential extent.

Abstractly, the related eccentric movement is conceived as a straight line going from one point (the universal mind) to another (the circumference) while simultaneously softening, kneading, and making the firm, unyielding, divided, formless matter ductile. Matter was easily influenced and it yielded to motives that enabled the universal mind to unite en masse and compose the different qualities of Maholalæl's faculty within it. This caused the effluvium to mutate effecting the similitudes power of being. Their evolution is disclosed in the following interpretation of *shemoneh* and *mœoth*.

Before rendering their meaning, let us pause for a moment and briefly discuss why every time "beings" are brought forth, the mass of creative waters are at their midst. It is because the elements of everything that is to exist are held in solution—in water. *Schamayim* (the kabbalistic name given to the creative waters) is "the divine fiery waters, the universal mercury—sometimes called Azoth—the measureless spirit of life. *Schamayim* is the 'Ocean of Spirit,' within which all created and uncreated things exist and by the life of which they are animated. *Schamayim* is the river of the living waters, the fiery source of all elements" (*The Secret Teachings of All Ages*, CXLV, CLV).

This short description of the creative waters will help the reader understand why their manipulation is always necessary when endeavoring to create the different faculties of the universal mind and their similitudes. The creative waters (elementary life) are indispensable for the manifestation of life. It plays an essential role in the history of creation and in the development of man.

Shemoneh reveals that the universal mind was taken for means or instrument to mobilize these waters and to draw from them elements that could be rendered images, representations, or similitudes of its faculty Maholalæl in material substance. Further, it reveals that the universal mind particularized the evolving similitudes by circumscribing their extent. This means that the similitudes were:

- endowed with all the specifications and detailed description of Maholalæl's attributes. That is to say, Maholalæl's similitudes were mighty and made to serve as an instrument of generative power to manifest in man the splendor, exaltation, and glory of the soul

- classified into sets, sorts, ranks, race, and genera
  - ○ sets. Maholalæl's similitudes were classified by type. They were endowed to each individual soul of man and not to any other groups of soul life (animals)
  - ○ sorts. The similitudes were classified as male and female. Male gender incorporated love, force, and intellect. Female gender contributed wisdom, higher emotions, and intuition
  - ○ ranks. The similitudes were placed in the highest division—mankind's—which is the highest manifestation of soul life on earth
  - ○ genera. Collectively, the similitudes resembled the faculty Maholalæl as opposed to any other faculty of the universal mind (Sheth, Ænôsh, or Kainan)

Their circumscription encompassed:

- describing them by their properties or peculiar qualities (i.e.: mental elevation and physical strengths);
- giving them their proper measure to ascertained their dimensions, which defined or reduced them to precision;
- assigning them with their corresponding number(s) to express their mathematical magnitude (precise amount) as in counting, especially (1) to indicate their position or number in a group or series or to provide a mark of identification (as one similitude may be given the number one because it was made first, and another may be given the number two because it was made second, and so on) and (2) to count the number of similitudes in a plurality in order to express their total;
- designating the limit to their extent;

- endowing them with a natural ability to rise up and shine; and
- qualifying them to exercise their function and to model the souls' uplifting endeavors

In short, circumscribing the extent of Maholalæl in the similitudes encompassed figuring, defining, and forming ideas, images, or models of this faculty. Moreover, the models were particularized; that is, they were given separate and distinct existences. But this particularization was in its infancy, and it resulted in a production of similitudes that were young and fragile tending in the direction in which or toward which the desire of the universal mind worked or moved. *Shemoneh* reveals that the similitudes grew to a great number. They were fattened, or made fertile and fruitful, unencumbered and free to develop to the extent of Maholalæl.

Mæôth makes known that extending, dilating, and manifesting the similitudes exteriorly were transitional movements that caused the universal mind to pass from one state of being into another bringing changes into its nature, essence, qualities, and attributes. *Shanah* reveals that these changes were universal and ontological mutations that culminated in bringing forth Maholalæl's similitudes.

EMANATION OF MAHOLALÆL'S SIMILITUDES

The Hebrew words *iôled banîm w-banôth* validate the universal mind emanated a great multitude of faculties resembling Maholalæl, the rising might and brightness of the universal mind. *Banîm w-banôth* reveals that these were male and female emanations. They were intelligible embodiments characterized by Maholalæl's circumscriptive extent. They were the sameness of Maholalæl designed to provide man with the power to rise up and shine, that is, to have mental elevation, greatness, dignity, splendor, glory, and great bodily strength.

SUMMARY

Genesis 5:16 discloses how the universal mind brought forth Maholalæl's similitudes, that through this mighty power man may develop his entire being, that through the development of this faculty he may reach the culminating point of his soul personality (or that which constitutes his lower nature) and rise up unto the heaven world. The verse also reveals the underlying meaning of the number 830, which communicates how the similitudes were developed.

★ PRACTICAL APPLICATION

This chapter briefly mentions the role of water in the history of creation and of man. It states that water is elemental, a primordial substance necessary for the manifestation of life. This helps us understand why water is necessary to sustain living organisms. We see that the manifestation of life begins in a water medium. For example, the sperm travels through a water medium to reach the egg, which is in a water medium, and then conception takes place in a water medium. That is to say, we humans are essentially aquatic beings, because we are conceived in water. *We are dependent on the life-giving properties of water.*

Studies show that the human body is composed primarily of water. It requires a great amount of water to conserve its health. Lack of water in our organism constitutes one of the fundamental causes of diseases and abnormalities. For instance, F. Batmanghelidj, MD, author of *Your Body's Many Cries for Water*, states: "High blood pressure (essential hypertension) is an adaptive process to a gross body water deficiency." He states, "When we do not drink enough water to serve all the needs of the body, some cells become dehydrated and lose some of their water to the circulation. The capillary beds in some areas will have to close so that some of the slack in capacity is adjusted. In water shortage and body drought, 66 percent is taken from the water volume normally held inside the cells; 26 percent is taken from the volume held outside the cells, and 8 percent is taken from blood volume. There is no alternative for the blood vessels other than closing their lumen to cope with the loss in blood volume" (p. 71). This translates into hypertension!

Dr. Batmanghelidj says that "strict and absolutely regular daily water intake prevents stresses and associated damages of dehydration" (p. 131). He states, "Chronic cellular dehydration painfully and prematurely kills. Its initial outward manifestations have until now been labeled as diseases of unknown origin" (p. X).

CRITICAL THINKING

1. According to the Hebrew word *îhî* mentioned in Genesis 5:16, the elements to compose Maholalæl's similitudes were rendered manifest and obvious in response to the impulsion of the universal mind upon elementary life. The manifestation of these elements enabled the universal mind to become conscious of its faculty Maholalæl serving in some capacity. Explain.

2. The Hebrew word *âhoreî* in Genesis 5:16 relates that elements were confined in order to give them forms or expressions that were compressed and centralized. Centralization of the elements brought reconciliation of two antagonistic forces surrounding the elements. Name the two forces.

---

3. The universal mind exercised its executive force upon the universal quaternary and upon its faculty Iared. In what capacity were these two forces helpful?

4. What is the meaning of the *circumferential extent*?

5. What must the universal mind do to manifest the necessary elements to build similitudes of its faculties and yield a real and evident existence?

6. To produce Maholalæl's similitudes in material substance necessitated to _____ the extent of Maholalæl's _____ in its similitudes.

7. The so-called "sons and daughters" of Maholalæl given in the Holy Bible are kabbalistically interpreted as the faculties that will enable man to _____and _____.

(Answers in Appendix B)

---

1. Refer to footnotes 1 and 2 in chapter 10.

17

MIGHT AND BRIGHTNESS FACULTY FOR THE SOULS OF MEN: MAHOLALÆL'S SIMILITUDES, PART 2

GENESIS 5:17

- Translation from the King James Version of the Bible: "And all the days of Mahalaleel were eight hundred ninety and five years and he died."
- Literal English translation as it appears in *The Hebraic Tongue Restored*: "And they were, all the days (manifested lights) of Mahollæl, five and nine tens of revolving-change and eight hundreds of revolution and he deceased."
- Transliteration from *The Hebraic Tongue Restored*: "Wa-îhîou chol îmeî Maholalæl hamesh w-thishahîm shanah w-shemoneh mæôth shanah wa-îamôth."

The following interpretation of Genesis 5:17 is spiritual in nature, not physical.

PROEM

The progression of Maholalæl's similitudes follows their birth. The previous chapter revealed that the universal mind emanated a great multitude of faculties resembling Maholalæl (the rising might and brightness faculty of the universal mind). We were told that these emanations were in their infancy and were therefore fragile, tending in the direction in which the universal mind worked or moved.

In this chapter, Genesis 5:17 informs us that after the similitudes were given agreeable forms they were advanced into a consolidated state to preserve them from loss. This conveys that the universal mind transformed the similitudes, as a natural process of universalizing their manifestation. The underlying meaning of the number 895 given in this verse elaborates on this transformation and gives additional details regarding the development of Maholalæl's similitudes.

UNDERLYING MEANING OF THE NUMBER 895

Hamesh, thishahîm, shemoneh, and *mœôth* are the Hebrew names composing the number 895. They were divided into their monosyllabic components and subsequently examined to unveil their meaning.

Hamesh (number five) conveys that (1) the universal mind exerted great effort upon elementary existence to manifest the necessary elements to build Maholalæl's similitudes, (2) by utilizing its formative faculty the universal mind made the elements palpable and compact. This enabled the universal mind to draw them from their depth, (3) By contractile movements the inwrapping of the elements were apprehended, and the heat that resulted (animation of the elements) was an effect of the contractile movements, (4) the passive and conditional casuality of the universal mind was activated upon apprehending the elements. It enabled the universal mind to receive impressions, which engaged its plastic power to fashion the elements in accordance with the impressions received.

Step-by-step the universal mind transformed (metamorphosed) the evolving similitudes into a consolidated state that preserved them from loss and kept them in an entire state. *Thishahîm* (number ninety) reveals that it was a gradual process of molding and carefully closing the similitudes' growth and material development, which had manifested universally.

Shemoneh (number eight) discloses how their universalization took place and how the extent of Maholalæl circumscription was convened into its similitudes. Chapter 16 gives a detailed exposition of this event.

Mæôth reveals that the manifestation of Maholalæl's similitudes was in harmony and accord with divine laws and it was a transitional movement leading to the transmutation of the universal mind.

TRANSMUTATION OF THE UNIVERSAL MIND

The Hebrew word *shanah* reveals that the transmutation occurred in cyclic changes that revolved around this passed period of activities. Once it ended, the universal mind returned to its state of seity from whence it had begun to move. *Shanah* reveals that at the end of this period of activity, the universal mind was not found in the same state as when Maholalæl was brought forth.

The Hebrew word *îamôth* reveals that the universal mind had transformed into a different way of being. The succeeding change came as a result of having grown in stature because of its new acquisitions—Iared and Maholalæl's similitudes. Iared gave the universal mind its powers of steadfastness and perseverance, and developing Maholalæl's similitudes enabled it to provide man with the ability to aggrandize and develop his being in its entirety—physically, mentally, morally, and spiritually.

SUMMARY

Genesis 5:17 reveals (1) how the universal mind exerted great force upon elementary existence to render the necessary elements to build Maholalæl's similitudes—the faculties that enables man to develop his being in its entirety: physically, mentally, morally and spiritually, (2) how those similitudes were advanced into a consolidated state to preserve them from loss and keep them in an entire state, and (3) how the transmutation of the universal mind ensued following this period of activity.

★ PRACTICAL APPLICATION

Genesis 5:17 reveals that man has been endowed with the power to aggrandize and develop his being in its entirety—physically, mentally, morally, and spiritually. Recognizing this inherent power can help us give expression to it.

Physically, we can endeavor to possess physical force, power, or energy, such as muscular force or vigor. We can endeavor to sustain the application of force without breaking or yielding, to be tough and have power of resistance, and to have the ability to bear and the capacity for exertion.

Mentally, we can endeavor to exert ourselves intellectually, to have power of mind, to be another Albert Einstein, to exercise memory, judgment, eloquence, or vigor of style, and to secure results in the fine arts.

Morally, we can endeavor to perform social duties, to be reasonable, to conform to rules of right or the accepted rules respecting social duties, to be a Martin Luther King Jr. or a Mahatma Gandhi, to be virtuous, just, and especially irreproachable in one's sexual relations, and to practice good manners or conduct.

Spiritually, we can endeavor to aggrandize our soul by allowing it to express itself in everything we do. We can let the soul guide us in our daily activities by listening to the voice of our conscience. We can endeavor to sustain our spirituality by learning spiritual truths designed to help us tread the path of swift unfoldment with no gaps in between. We can include all experiences and their fruits in a concentrated form of living, for only in this way may the totality of advancement be achieved and the exaltation of the soul be procured.

CRITICAL THINKING

1. Genesis 5:17 disclosed the next step in the advancement of Maholalæl's similitudes. What is this next step?
2. After developing Maholalæl's similitudes the universal mind transformed into a different way of being. Why?

(Answers in Appendix B)

18

CENTRAL MIGHT AND PANGING QUALITIES OF THE UNIVERSAL MIND: HENOCH

GENESIS 5:18

- Translation from the King James Version of the Bible: "And Jared lived an hundred sixty and two years and he begat Enoch."
- The literal English translation as it appears in *The Hebraic Tongue Restored*: "And he lived, Ired, two and six-tens of revolving change, and one hundred of revolution; and he begat the selfsameness of Henoch (the central might, and also the panging one)."
- Transliteration from *The Hebraic Tongue Restored*: "Wa-îhî Iared Shethaîm w'shishîm shanah w' mæôth shanah wa-iôled æth Hanoch."

The following interpretation of Genesis 5:18 is spiritual in nature, not physical.

PROEM

The beginning of a new period of activity is marked by the advent of a new faculty. This new faculty will enable the universal mind to finish corporeal being. Accordingly, Genesis 5:18 reveals that possessing the faculty Iared enabled the universal mind to bring forth its new power, *Henoch* (Enoch).

Henoch represents corporeal force at the center of being. The Hebrew text reveals that Henoch influenced by the posterity of Sheth can also be taken figuratively to mean, "panging qualities" (repentance and contrition).

Making this new faculty requires extracting elements from elementary existence (the creative waters), and subsequently, molding them into the new faculty. The Hebrew word *îhî* concurs with this knowledge.

Extracting these elements enabled the universal mind to become conscious of conditions pertaining to its faculty Iared supplying the means to move the elements downward into the sphere of activity, in turn, enabling it to build its new faculty in substance. The number 162 given in this verse conveys the story.

UNDERLYING MEANING OF THE NUMBER 162

Shethaîm, *Shishîm*, and *Mæoth* are the three Hebrew names composing the number 162. Each name was examined individually to access its underlying meaning.

Shethaîm (number two) contains all ideas of mutation, transition, passing from one state to another, and redundancy. Accordingly, number two conveys that the downward movement of the elements into the sphere of activity is associated with a transition or change that the elements underwent as they were passed from one state of development into another. This produced a real and evident existence, which according to *shishîm* (number sixty) it acquainted the universal mind with certain properties and states pertaining to its new faculty appearing in substance. It conveys that the evolving faculty was substantialized in proportional measures and was made to resemble the universal mind, fitted and suitable to be developed universally.

The Hebrew words *shanah* and *mæôth* reveal that the evolving faculty was passed from one state to another in accords with the universal mind's desire to manifest the faculty exteriorly. This was a transitional movement that led the universal mind to mutate repeatedly. *Shanah* tells us that mutations—which caused a change in the nature, essence, qualities, and attributes of the universal mind, and which transformed it in form—enabled the universal mind to bring forth its new faculty either in the order of things, or in the order of time relative to its diverse mutations.

A NEW FACULTY IS BORN

The Hebrew words *iôled æth-Hanoch* reiterate that the changes undergone by the universal mind resulted in bringing forth its new faculty, which Moses named Henoch—the universal mind's central might and panging qualities. With this new faculty, the universal mind brought forth its centralization power, or ability to draw things to a central point enabling it to combine or concentrate several parts into a whole (likened to the parts of the human body brought together to function as a whole). The Hebrew text reveals that Henoch is the central power or force at the center of being, the corporate force. Figuratively, *Henoch* may mean "repentance and contrition," or "a pang."

HENOCH IS KAIN (CAIN) DILUTED

The Hebrew text discloses that the name *Henoch* (or *Enoch* as written in the Bible) is presented here with all the force it has in the posterity of Kain, the strong and mighty force, which lies in the center of being and which assumes and assimilates to itself. Henoch is that same central power, the same corporate force, but the posterity of Sheth influences the moral idea it contains. Henoch can then be considered to be in relationship with repentance and contrition. The pressure—literally, the shock—that it expresses can be taken figuratively, and it becomes a pang. A pang is characterized by extreme pain, anguish, agony of body, deep sorrow for sin, and the grief of heart felt when one does wrong by exercising vices and weaknesses.

Henoch is the founder (builder); the central might, essentially, a faculty fit in physical qualities. It is elementary in its rudimentary beginning, arresting, seizing on, and fixing the finished corporeal being (*Ænôsh*), which is now influenced by the posterity of Sheth under the relationship of repentance and contrition. Possessing this faculty enables corporeal man to repent and be contrite for vices and weaknesses inherent in his physical faculties.

HIEROGLYPHIC MEANING OF THE NAME *HENOCH*

As Corporeal Existence

Hieroglyphically, *Henoch* is rendered as: elementary existence, which characterizes a real corporeal existence that passes from one nature to another and agglomerates or gathers into a mass. It solidifies the assimilative reflective and transient life of corporeal man. This is the life that mirrors its source ("as above, so below"), and it is fleeting in its physical existence.

Without distinction or preference, corporeal existence communicates, imparts, or bestows to all forms of corporeal man (tall, short, dwarf, wide, thin, black, white, mulatto, yellow, red races, and so on) its virtues and vices, weaknesses and strengths.

As Panging Qualities

Considered as a pang (repentance and contrition), *Henoch* can also be rendered as "every effort and every difficult and painful action." It is the image of keen pain or anguish excited by a sense of guilt (remorse or self-reproach). Further, it expresses the idea of prayer, of supplication, of that which is exorable or moved by entreaty (urgent prayer or earnest petition) and which allows itself to relent. It is a grace to grant or to be granted, as a favor. It is that which is clement, merciful, kind, and full of pity. It is sacrifice, a rendering sacred.

On the other hand, *Henoch* can in like manner be injurious to existence, as it arrests the senses, or hinders the motion of thoughts. It restrains being. It represses it. It is likened to a blow to the egocentric. It torments. It rebukes or afflicts for correction. It chastises and treats harshly. It punishes, bruises, and strikes self-centeredness.

ADAM'S MICROCOSM (7/10)

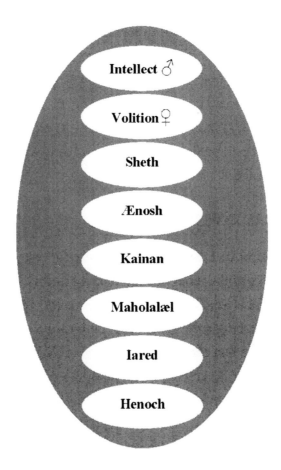

Figure 18.1 above depicts the addition of Henoch to the growing faculties of Adam (universal mind). His microcosm is now composed of intellect (male principle), volition/will (female principle), Sheth (Adam's power to frame the foundation of the soul), Ænosh (Adam's physical faculties, corporeal man), Kainan (Adam's general invading force), Maholalæl (Adam's rising might and brightness), Iared (Adam's power of steadfastness and perseverance), and Henoch (Adam's corporate force and panging qualities).

SUMMARY

Genesis 5:18 reveals the generation of a new faculty, Henoch. The Hebrew text discloses that Henoch represents corporeal force at the center of being, but it is influenced by the posterity of Sheth. As a result, Henoch can also be taken figuratively to mean, "panging qualities." In addition, Henoch is the builder; the central might at the core of being. It is essentially a faculty fit into physical qualities, elementary in its rudimentary beginning, arresting, seizing on, and fixing the finished corporeal man.

★ PRACTICAL APPLICATION

This chapter introduced the advent of *Henoch*, the central might and panging qualities of the universal mind. Genesis 5:18 revealed that this central might is the corporate force at the center of being, while panging qualities are considered to be repentance and contrition. We can readily discern that exercising the "panging side" of this faculty gives man a chance to repent, to feel contrition for wrongdoing, which leads to the amendment of life.

CRITICAL THINKING

1. Genesis 5:18 revealed the generation of a new faculty. What is the name of this new faculty?

2. For what purpose was this faculty created?

3. Rendering the elements to build its new faculty made the universal mind conscious of its faculty *Iared*. What did the universal mind become conscious of?

4. The universal development of this new faculty was dependent upon passing elements from one state to another and evolving them into the new faculty. What else must happen in order for the universal mind to bring forth this new faculty?

5. Henoch is the same central power, the same corporate force as that of Kain (Cain), but being influenced by the posterity of Sheth, the moral idea, which Henoch contains, is that of _____ and _____.

6. Henoch is a faculty fit into the physical qualities of _____ ____.

7. The faculty Henoch can transform the vices and weaknesses inherent in the faculty Ænôsh (corporeal man) through _____ and _____.

(Answers in Appendix B)

19

STEADFASTNESS AND PERSEVERANCE: DUAL ABILITIES FOR THE SOULS OF MEN, PART 1

GENESIS 5:19

- Translation from the King James Version of the Bible: "And Jared lived after he begat Enoch eight hundred years and begat sons and daughters."
- The literal English translation as it appears in *The Hebraic Tongue Restored*: "And he lived, Ired, after the causing him to beget that same Henoch, eight hundreds of revolving change; and he begat sons and daughters (many issued offspring)."
- Transliteration from *The Hebrew Tongue Restored*: "Wa-îhî Iared âhoreî hôlid-ô æth-Hanôch shemoneh mæôth shanah: wa-îôled banîm w-banôth."

The following interpretation of Genesis 5:19 is spiritual in nature, not physical.

PROEM

Bringing forth the similitudes of Iared for the benefit of the souls is in the order of things for the universal mind. Recall that Iared is the "steadfast" and "persevering" dual faculty of the universal mind. Genesis 5:19 reveals that Iared is to serve as the model from which its similitudes (or symbolical sons and daughters) will be fashioned.

Iared's similitudes will enable the souls of men to steadily move upward in the ascension process (via evolution) or move downward in the involution process. The upward movement will enable souls to ascend to the Ideal from which they emanated, with enhanced powers and virtues. The downward movement will enable souls to involve their qualities and potencies in matter, thereby limiting themselves in form so that their qualities can unfold while encased in the human body.

BUILDING IARED'S SIMILITUDES

We learned from previous chapters that in building similitudes the universal mind must first manifest elements (protons, electrons, and other constituent ingredients) and subsequently build the similitudes from the elements. The Hebrew word *îhî* reveals in addition that upon manifesting the elements, the universal mind became conscious of its steadfast and persevering power enabling it to equilibrate and equalize every junction, adjunction, and reconciliation made upon the elements in order to build Iared's similitudes.

The Hebrew word *âhoreî* reveals that equilibrating and equalizing the elements required stabilizing, compacting, and centralizing the elements. Concentric movements (made by the universal mind), which compacted the elements, accomplished their centralization. Centralization caused an effluvium (ethereal, spirituous emanations of the evolving similitudes) to manifest.

The effluvium was the manifestation of the similitudes' potential life or power of being. The Hebrew word *hôlid* reveals that Iared's similitudes, which did not yet exist, were found, nevertheless, to have the power to exist. Their power to exist unfolded as the universal mind passed the effluvium from one nature to another in an eccentric movement designed to extend, rise, and unfold the effluvium in all directions within its sphere of activity.

ECCENTRIC MOVEMENT OF THE UNIVERSAL MIND

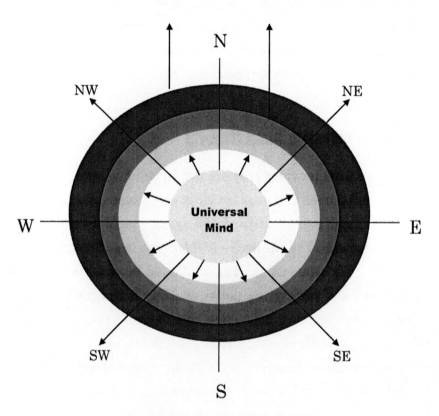

SPHERE OF ACTIVITY

Figure 19.1 above depicts the eccentric movement of the universal mind within its sphere of activity. The universal mind is portrayed dispersing the effluvium (represented by the arrows) in all directions: east, west, north, south, southeast, southwest, northeast, northwest, and depth.

Hôlid conveys that the eccentric movement expanded the intellectual powers of the universal mind. With this expansion, the universal mind apprehended how to progressively build Iared's similitudes: from combining elements to make atoms, to joining atoms to create coalitions that united them into a mass. This necessitated the universal mind to activate the universal quaternary[1] and its centralization power (Henoch) to enable it to solidify the mass (the evolving similitudes).

The following interpretation of the number eight hundred given in this verse conveys the progression of the evolving similitudes.

UNDERLYING MEANING OF THE NUMBER 800

We will begin the interpretation of the number eight hundred by examining its two components: *shemoneh* (number eight) and *mâoth* (number one hundred).

Shemoneh reveals that the universal mind universalized the evolving similitudes at the circumferential extent (the entire sphere of activity). This was a sort of movement by which the universal mind was instrumental in mobilizing the passive, creative waters to draw elements from their depth, and subsequently, to render them into images, representations, or similitudes of its faculty Iared in material substance.

Shemoneh discloses that the similitudes circumscribed the extent of Iared. They characterized all specifications or descriptions of Iared's attributes—the steadfast and persevering power that enable the souls of men to involve their qualities and potencies into matter and to move them upward in the ascension process through evolution.

Further, *shemoneh* inform us that the similitudes were classified into sets, sorts, ranks, and genera:

- sets. The similitudes were classified by type. That is, Iared's similitudes were endowed to the souls of men and not to any other soul life.
- sorts. The similitudes were sorted by gender: male and female similitudes.
- ranks. The similitudes were placed in the highest division among soul life—mankind's.
- genera. The similitudes collectively resembled the faculty Iared. They were differentiated from any other faculty possessed by the universal mind (Sheth, Ænosh, Kainan, or Maholalæl).

The similitudes' circumscription encompassed:

- describing them by their properties or peculiar qualities, such as possessing the power to persist in anything undertaken; having the power to govern, to predominate over, to influence most prominently, to have the greatest effect upon, to give specific character to, or to overshadow;
- giving them their proper measure, which ascertained their dimensions and reduced them to precision;
- assigning them with their number(s) to express their mathematical magnitude or precise amount, as in counting, and to indicate their position in a group or series or as a mark of identification (i.e., the first production of Iared's similitudes may be given the number one; the second, number two, and so on);
- establishing all determinations or boundaries to their extent;

- stipulating all qualifications that they may exercise their function; and
- endowing them with the ability to adapt to the uses of the soul.

Shemoneh conveys that the above conglomerate of works were the actions of giving determinate forms (extent) to Iared's similitudes and of particularizing their existence, though they were rudimentary in their stage of development. It further conveys that the evolving similitudes grew to a great number. They were made fertile and fruitful, unencumbered and free to develop to the extent of Iared.

Mæôth tells us that manifesting the similitudes was in sympathy with divine laws and it was a transitional movement that led the universal mind to mutate over and over as it endeavored to bring forth the similitudes.

The Hebrew word *shanah* reveals that these repeated mutations effected a change in the nature, essence, qualities, and attributes of the universal mind and it altered it in form, thereby enabling it to emanate Iared's similitudes either in the order of things, or in the order of time relative to its diverse mutations.

BRINGING FORTH IARED'S SIMILITUDES

The Hebrew words *iôled banîm w-banôth* confirm that the universal mind emanated many offspring resembling Iared. Iared's similitudes proceeded from potentiality in action, from every manifestation of generative action coming from the universal mind. The offspring were intelligible embodiments characterized by Iared's circumscriptive extent and definition of Iared's inclosing boundaries. They were the sameness of Iared and constituted the sum total of Iared's faculty, providing the souls of men with dual abilities: steadfastness and perseverance to descend and involute their qualities into matter and to ascend from matter (via evolution) into the higher realms of existence with enhanced powers and virtues gained from experience while incased in matter (their physical forms).

SUMMARY

Genesis 5:19 reveals the particulars leading to the development of Iared's similitudes, the "steadfast and persevering" faculty of the souls, which enables them to descend and involute their qualities into matter and to ascend from matter via evolution into higher realms of existence with enhanced powers and virtues gained from experience while incase in their physical form.

★ PRACTICAL APPLICATION

We involute our potential qualities in matter so that we can evolve them from matter with enhanced powers and virtues resulting from having developed ourselves through our experiences on earth. Through evolution, we gradually emerge into objective activity (unfold) the qualities and faculties we possess. As we evolve, we begin to rise from matter and eventually discard our physical body when there is no more to learn in the physical plane. Ancient teachings reveal that, after discarding our physical vehicle, we return to our original state, having gained the experience, wisdom, and fruitage of all our personal lives (incarnations).

Steadfastness and perseverance are crucial in the ascension process. These powers keep our mind focused on treading the path of swift unfoldment. On the other hand, if we desire to pursue worldly endeavors, we must utilize that same faculty of steadfastness and perseverance to attain our goals on earth. After we have fulfilled all of our mundane desires, we start focusing our mind upward toward the divine. Once this point is reached, there is generally no laxity of continued perusal and unfolding. The depth of understanding will come by steadfastly studying and attuning our mind with the mind of the divine.

CRITICAL THINKING

1. Genesis 5:19 revealed the particulars leading to the emanation of Iared's similitudes, the souls' faculty of steadfastness and perseverance. For what purpose was this faculty endowed to the souls?
2. Describe three properties or peculiar qualities that may be exhibited by the similitudes of Iared.

(Answers in Appendix B)

---

l. *Quaternary*—Refer to footnote 3 in chapter 10.

20

STEADFASTNESS AND PERSEVERANCE: DUAL ABILITIES FOR THE SOULS OF MEN, PART 2

GENESIS 5:20

- Translation from the King James Version of the Bible: "And all the days of Jared were nine hundred sixty and two years and he died."
- The literal English translation as it appears in *The Hebraic Tongue Restored*: "And they were, all the days, (manifested lights) of Ired, two and six-tens of revolving change, and nine hundreds of revolution, and he deceased."
- Transliteration from *The Hebraic Tongue Restored*: "Wa îhîou chol-îemeî Iared shethîm w-shishîm shanah w-theshah mæoth shanah wa-îamôth."

The following interpretation of Genesis 5:20 is spiritual in nature, not physical.

PROEM

We learned in previous chapters that arranging, preparing, and giving agreeable forms to similitudes of faculties advances (accelerates) all movements of the eternally living waters where elements—or the simplest constituent principles of which anything consists—are held in solution. Giving agreeable forms to Iared's similitudes during their luminous period of manifestation is no different. The living waters were quickened to manifest elements, and subsequently, to render them into the similitudes. The Hebrew words *îhîou chol îemeî Iared* in Genesis 5:20 reveal this knowledge and the underlying meaning of the number 962 gives additional details.

UNDERLYING MEANING OF THE NUMBER 962

The Hebrew names *shethîm, shishîm, theshah,* and *mæoth* represent the number 962. Their examination reveals how Iared's similitudes were given reality and how this was a transitional movement that led the universal mind to transmute.

Shethîm (number two) reveals that the universal mind universalized the similitudes as they were passed from one state of development into another effecting a real and evident existence that was manifested in substance. *Shishîm* (number sixty) conveys that their reality was conceived principally under the relationship of:

- proportion (Iared's similitudes were symmetrically arranged.)
- measure (Iared's similitudes were given dimensions, which reduced them to precision.)
- harmony (Iared's similitudes were fitted for their role.)
- equality (Iared's similitudes were evenly uniformed.)
- equilibrium (Iared's similitudes were evenly balanced.)
- parallelism (Iared's similitudes were similar in construction; they resembled each other.)
- fitness (Iared's similitudes were suitable and adaptable to develop universally.)

Moreover, *theshah* (number nine) reveals that the boundaries, designations, definitions, and measures of the similitudes were influenced as they passed from one state of development to another. This tells us that the Law of Continuity and Reciprocity—which states that nothing passes from one state to another without passing through all its intermediate states—was in operation. It denotes that the universal mind gradually transformed or consolidated the similitudes to preserve their constituent parts from loss. It was a gradual process that cemented, guaranteed, and plastered the similitudes, and consequently, molded, shaped, and carefully closed their animated matter. Iared's similitudes had quickened as a result of the consolidating and plastering actions of the universal mind. *Mæôth* reveals that this ends a period of activity and distinguishes a period of transition for the universal mind. In succession, the universal mind transmuted or changed its mode of existing.

TRANSMUTATION OF THE UNIVERSAL MIND

Shanah discloses that the universal mind transmuted in cyclic revolutions that coincided with the beginning and ending period of these recent activities. Accordingly, these revolutions brought the universal mind back to its state of seity, the state from whence it had begun to move, likened to making a 360-degree turn. *Shanah* reveals that the universal mind was not found at the end of this period of activity in the same state that it was at its beginning when it embarked to produce Henoch and the similitudes of Iared. The Hebrew word *îamôth* discloses that the universal mind had transformed into a different way of being, a succeeding change that came under the Law of Cause and Effect. The production of Iared's similitudes and of its centralization might and panging qualities (Henoch) served as causes. Transforming into a different way of being was the effect.

SUMMARY

Genesis 5:20 reveals how Iared's similitudes were given reality, how the Law of Continuity and Reciprocity affected the similitudes, and how the universal mind transmuted into a different way of being after having completed this period of activities.

★ *PRACTICAL APPLICATION*

Genesis 5:20 revealed the metamorphosing of Iared's similitudes (the dual faculty of steadfastness and perseverance for the souls of men). Just as the universal mind steadfastly persevered to metamorphose the similitudes, so we must willfully execute this faculty, which is endowed to each human soul, as a preliminary step to attain goals in the material and spiritual worlds. One must not yield to reason, or be moved from one's notions, inclinations, and purposes by counsel, advice, commands, instructions, etc., if we are to attain. A wish alone will not accomplish our goals, for a wish is a helpless desire of the mind. A desire alone will not do it, for desire—though a little stronger than a wish—is often followed by fitful efforts to manifest itself into action, but that is all.

Then comes determination. Here we intend to attain. However, though stronger than desire and often expressed very forcefully once or twice through action, determination is often discouraged after one—or perhaps several—unsuccessful efforts. It takes our volitive faculty (our female principle) to begin to perform a series of continuous, undiscourageable, unceasing determinations and acts revolving around our desire, until our acts become dynamic enough to produce the much-craved result. This translates into steadfastly persevering with action until our goals are achieved.

CRITICAL THINKING

1. In this chapter, we learned that Iared's similitudes (the dual faculty of steadfastness and perseverance of the souls) were arranged, prepared, and given agreeable forms during their period of manifestation. What effect did this activity have upon the eternally living waters, which hold in solution the elements of anything that is to exist?
2. What happened to the universal mind after metamorphosing Iared's similitudes?
3. What activated the transformation of the universal mind?

(Answers in Appendix B)

21

THE EAGER SHAFT OF DEATH: METHOÛSHALAH

GENESIS 5:21

- Translation from the King James Version of the Bible: "And Enoch lived sixty and five years and begat Methuselah."
- The literal English translation as it appears in *The Hebraic Tongue Restored*: "And he endured, Henoch, five and six-tens of revolving change and he begat Methushalah (eager shaft of death)."
- Transliteration from The Hebraic Tongue Restored: "Wa îhî Hanôch hamesh w'shishîm shanah wa-îôled æth Methoûshalah."

The following interpretation of Genesis 5:21 is spiritual in nature, not physical.

PROEM

In chapter 18, we learned that the faculty Iared enabled the universal mind to bring forth its central might and "panging" qualities, a faculty Moses named *Henoch*.

Henoch now supplies the means to bring forth another faculty, the "eager shaft of death," Methoûshalah. This faculty will enable the souls of men to swiftly hurl upward toward the eternity of existence upon transition or so-called death. Further, the Hebrew text conveys that Moses made a distinction between this kind of death and the kind of death that precipitates, hastens without preparation, or throws headlong from a height, devouring, destroying, and consuming wantonly and with violence. This kind of death is known as Methoushael, the "gulf or abyss of death" (Genesis 4:18).

Genesis 5:21 begins by disclosing the impulsions of the universal mind upon elementary existence rendered elements manifest and obvious. Rendering these elements enabled the universal mind to become conscious of its centralization power (Henoch) furnishing the mean to bring forth Methoûshalah. Moses used the number 65 to veil the activities leading to the production of this faculty.

UNDERLYING MEANING OF THE NUMBER 65

Hamesh and *shishîm* are the two Hebrew names composing the number 65. Close examination of the Hebrew roots and signs forming these names uncovered their underlying meaning.

Hamesh (number five) reveals that great effort was exerted upon elementary existence (the creative waters) to manifest the necessary elements to build the new faculty. These were rapid, powerful contractile movements made inside the waters to solidify and draw the elements to the surface. It made them palpable and compact, which enabled the universal mind to pull them from their depth. The powerful contractile movements cause heat to emanate from the elements. This was the animation or excitation that wakened the elements from sleep or repose and roused them into action.

THE FORMATIVE FACULTY OF THE UNIVERSAL MIND

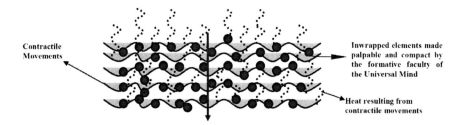

Contractile Movements

Inwrapped elements made palpable and compact by the formative faculty of the Universal Mind

Heat resulting from contractile movements

DEPTH OF ELEMENTARY EXISTENCE

Figure 21.1 above depicts the formative faculty of the universal mind mobilizing the creative waters, where the elements of all things that are to exist are held in solution. It shows contractile movements making elements palpable and compact and the heat oozing out from the excitation of the elements.

Hamesh further reveals that the universal mind passively received impressions upon coming in contact with the elements enabling it to have a mental image of its evolving new faculty. In succession, the plastic power of the universal mind fashioned the elements according to the impressions received and a real and evident existence was manifested.

Shishîm (number sixty) reveals that the new existence was given (1) proportion in regards to the arrangement of its constituent parts; (2) measure to reduce it to precision; (3) harmony to give it symmetry; (4) uniformity to have consistency; (5) equilibrium to remain firm, balanced; (6) parallelism to have all essential parts resembling its maker; and (7) fitness or adaptability to enable it to develop universally.

A NEW FACULTY IS BORN

To manifest and develop the faculty universally required the universal mind to change its nature, essence, qualities, and attributes. *Shanah* reveals these changes were universal and ontological mutations that altered the universal mind in form thereby enabling it to bring forth its new faculty, Methoûshalah, the "eager shaft of death."

TWO KINDS OF DEATH: *METHOÛSHALAH* AND *METHOUSHAEL*

Methoûshalah was first introduced by Moses in Genesis 4:18 (not covered in this book) in the posterity of Kain. In Genesis 5:21, the change brought into this name is hardly perceptible. Fabre d'Olivet states that the root *Moth* or "death" always constitutes its foundation. The word *shalah*, which was added to the root, signifies literally a dart. In the posterity of Kain, *Methoushael* symbolizes the "gulf" (or "abyss") of death, a death that precipitates or hastens without preparation; that throws headlong or down from a height, that devours or destroys, consuming wantonly and with violence. This death annihilates.

However, in the posterity of Sheth, *Methoûshalah* characterizes the *dart* of death—that is, a so-called death that, at transition, swiftly hurls souls or moves them rapidly toward the eternity of existence. Thus Moses admits to two kinds of death, and according to Fabre d'Olivet, this is worthy of notice.

Tranquil and Happy Existence

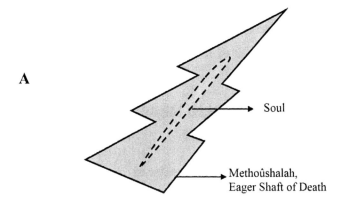

At transition the soul is taken either upward or downward

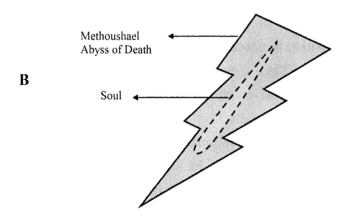

Fathomless Pit

In figure 21.2 above, figure *A* depicts the "eager shaft of death" (Methoûshalah) swiftly hurling a soul upward upon transition into the tranquil, happy, and orderly existence, which is in the way of salvation or safety from destruction. Figure *B* depicts death's "fathomless pit," with the abyss of death (Methoushael) precipitating or hastening a soul without preparation and throwing it headlong or down from a height to a gulf that is open and ready to swallow up, devour, destroy, consume wantonly and with violence, and annihilate. It is likened to the saying: "The wicked shall be cut off from the earth, and the transgressor shall be rooted out of it" (Proverbs 2:22).

HIEROGLYPHIC AND SYMBOLIC MEANING OF THE NAME *METHOÛSHALAH*

Hieroglyphically, *Methoûshalah* is rendered as a sympathetic movement or transition that transmutes souls into a different way of existence, changes souls from one nature or substance into another, and passes souls into the *occult*,[1] *profound*,[2] and *unknown*[3] existence.

Symbolically, *Methoûshalah* represents an expansive movement that extends, rises, and unfolds the souls. It follows divine laws and directs souls toward their initial existence. It represents souls being passed from one nature to another on the ascending curved line of the sphere of activity. This is a quick moving of souls to that which is tranquil, happy, in good order, and in the way of salvation or preservation from destruction.

In the involutionary and evolutionary processes of life, the soul descends into matter and ascends to higher states respectively. Involution restrains the soul in transitory forms (mental, emotional, astral, and physical vehicles of consciousness) for the purpose of becoming gradually expanded (unfolded). When its vehicles are discarded at the end of the soul's involutionary cycle—that is, when the soul passes through "transition"—it returns to its original blissful state with enhanced powers and virtues gained while involved in its transitory forms.

This is a turning movement, a change of the soul's position that occurs over and over in accordance with a definite plan. It continues to unfold until the *lesser day*[4] when the soul is liberated from the *wheel of necessity*[5]. This process is called "revolutions of the soul."

Genesis 5:21 discloses that the transition, or passing from one place or state to another, is made possible via Methoûshalah. Methoûshalah is a transitional movement. It is a faculty that enables the soul to transmute at the end of each involutionary cycle.

REVOLUTIONS OF THE SOUL

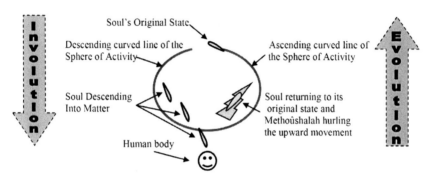

PHYSICAL PLANE

Figure 21.3 above depicts the revolutions of the soul. Methoûshalah is shown here facilitating the upward movement of a soul at transition.

Edna E. Craven

ADAM'S MICROCOSM (8/10)

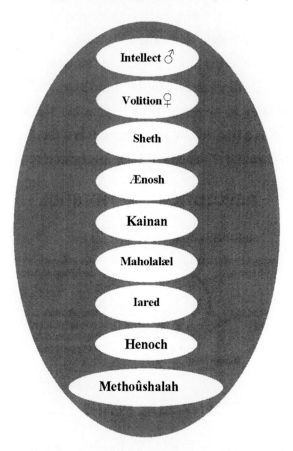

Figure 21.4 above depicts the addition of Methoûshalah to the unfolding microcosm of the universal mind (Adam). The growing faculties of Adam within his microcosm are now composed of intellect (Adam's male principle), volition/will (Adam's female principle), Sheth (Adam's power to frame the foundation of the soul), Ænosh (Adam's physical faculties, corporeal man), Kainan (Adam's general invading force), Maholalæl (Adam's rising might and brightness), Iared (Adam's powers of steadfastness and perseverance), Henoch (Adam's corporate force and panging qualities), and Methoûshalah (Adam's "eager shaft of death).

SUMMARY

Genesis 5:21 reveals how the faculty Henoch enabled the universal mind to bring forth another faculty, Methoûshalah, the "eager shaft of death." It reveals that Methoûshalah is the kind of death that swiftly hurls souls toward the eternity of existence upon transition, or the so-called death. This verse also reveals that there is another kind of death: the "gulf or abyss of death," which precipitates or hastens without preparation; that throws headlong or down from a height, that devours or destroys, consuming wantonly and with violence.

★ *PRACTICAL APPLICATION*

What happens to the soul after transition, or the so-called death, has provoked much interest for millennia. Genesis 5:21 reveals that the soul returns, over and over, to its original, blissful state after each transition. Ancient philosophies makes known that this is a process by which the soul unfolds while inhabiting transitory forms and then returns to its original state of rest after transition. In other words, the consciousness (soul) discards its vehicles at death and ascends through the various planes of existence in an order that reverses the way it descended.

The soul discards its vehicles of consciousness of the lower nature and spends a period of rest in *Devachan* (the home of the gods). Here, ancient teachings reveal the soul fully enjoys the fruits of the good deeds it performed while inhabiting its physical form during the preceding earth life. Thereafter, a new cycle opens, and a new physical incarnation begins for the soul. This is called *revolutions of the soul*, or the doctrine of reincarnation, also known as *Gilgoolem* in Hebrew.

The doctrine of reincarnation makes us cognizant that there is plenty of time to achieve all and to be joyous. It reveals that reincarnation is expedient and instinctive. Reincarnation is expedient, because it gives us a chance to atone for our mishaps, to make retribution, or to realize in another life the ideals that we never had time to realize in the life just left behind. Reincarnation is instinctive, because the impelling force that causes us to struggle to live makes us reluctant to admit or accept the belief that all must end at death.

CRITICAL THINKING

1. Genesis 5:21 reveals that a new faculty was brought forth by the universal mind. What is the name of this new faculty and what does it do?
2. According to the Hebrew text, how many kinds of deaths did Moses admit?
3. The "gulf" or "abyss" of death differs from the "eager shaft of death in what sense?
4. What is the foundation of Methoûshalah ("eager shaft of death")?
5. Methoûshalah is also known as _____.
6. What is the symbolic meaning of Methoûshalah?

(Answers in Appendix B)

---

1. *Occult existence*: an existence hidden from the eye or understanding, it is mysterious.

2. *Profound existence*: a humble existence, submissive to the divine will.

3. *Unknown existence*: a kind of life that is undiscovered; undetected; concealed.

4. *Lesser day*: when the soul returns to its cause or origin.

5. *Wheel of Necessity*: the periodic descent of the soul into incarnation, and the ascent therefrom. Wheel of Necessity is also known as "Wheels of Birth and Death" (GAG, 812).

22

HENOCH WALKED WITH GOD. SIMILITUDES OF HENOCH, PART 1

GENESIS 5:22

- Translation from the King James Version of the Bible: "And Enoch walked with God after he begat Methuselah three hundred years and begat sons and daughters."
- The literal English translation as it appears in *The Hebraic Tongue Restored*: "And he trod, Henoch, (in the steps) of HIM the Gods, after the causing him to beget that same Methushalah, three hundreds of revolving change; and he begat sons and daughters (many issued offspring)."
- Transliteration from *The Hebraic Tongue Restored*: "Wa-îthehallech Hanôch æth-ha-Ælohîm âhoreî hôlid-ô æth-Methoûshalah, shelosh mæôth shanah wa-îôled banîm w-banôth."

The following interpretation of Genesis 5:22 is spiritual in nature, not physical.

PROEM

In chapter 18 the advent of the faculty Henoch was made known. We were told that Henoch represents the universal mind's centralization power and the corporeal force at the center of being, but that influenced by the posterity of Sheth, Henoch can also be considered panging qualities. In this chapter Henoch is brought to light again. Genesis 5:22 reveals that *"Henoch walked with God"* and announces the advent of Henoch's similitudes (its symbolical sons and daughters).

In Hebrew, the phrase "walked with God" literally signifies "to be carried in every sense, to go to and to come." Thus Genesis 5:22 reveals that the meaning of *Henoch* ought to be taken more in a moral sense rather than in a more physical aspect. "Walked with God" conveys that Henoch is the faculty that enables the universal mind to follow the commandments or orders set by the Ælohîm.[1]

The commandments, intended as authoritative rules of action, were applied particularly to moral conduct, laws, instructions, injunctions, and maxims (chief premises or established principles). These carried the universal mind, in every sense, to and fro in two opposed movements that were *concentric* (moving toward the center[2]) to receive instructions, and *eccentric* (moving away from the center) for the purpose of manifesting every demonstrable and determined moral existence within its sphere of activity.

TREADING THE PATH

Genesis 5:22 begins with the Hebrew words *Wa-îthehallech*, which literally mean "and he trod." Let us examine this phrase. *Trod* is the verb *hallech*. *Hallech* is used here according to the reciprocal form (going backward and forward), literally signifying "to be carried in every sense and to go and come." This action, which Moses attributes to Henoch, proves that the meaning of this name ought to be taken in a more moral sense as descendant of Sheth (Seth), rather than in a more physical sense as the descendant of Kain. (Refer to *Henoch is Kain (Cain) Diluted* in chapter 18.)

The two roots that compose the Hebrew verb *hallech*—*hl* and *ach*—depict two opposed movements, eccentric (*hl*) and concentric (*ach*), going away and drawing near. According to *Strong's Concordance* (1980) the verb *trod* or *hallech* means "to walk." In a great variety of applications, both literal and figurative, Strong's states that it means "apace," "about," "abroad," "along," "away," "forward," "on," "out," "up and down," and "to and fro." *Gesenius' Lexicon* adds to these meanings by saying that *hallech* also means "the place one is going," "to follow anyone's footsteps," and "to imitate him in life and manners"—hence, *to follow the precepts of God*.

With the above-described understanding, we can now literally derive the following. Developing the faculty Henoch enabled the universal mind to follow the commandments or orders set by the Ælohîm, the unity of the Gods. The "to" and "fro" opposed movements are forces giving direction to moral life.

Îthehallech reveals:

- a directing power (Ælohîm) that serves to manifest (1) all determinations adhering to aims or purposes; (2) all designations given to the commandments to distinguish them from each other; and (3) all definitions given to the commandments applicable to their particular purpose;
- the signification of every evident, demonstrated, and determined moral existence, which shows itself by invincible and conclusive evidence; and

- an extensive movement springing from two opposed motions: *concentric*, which draws near to, and *eccentric*, which goes away from.

TWO OPPOSED MOTIONS GIVING DIRECTION TO LIFE

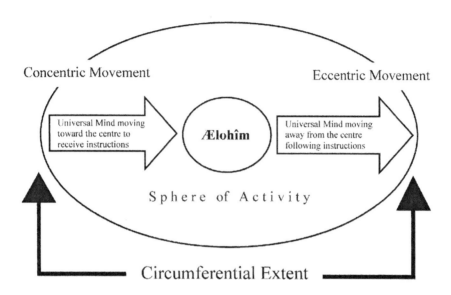

Concentric Movement

Eccentric Movement

Universal Mind moving toward the centre to receive instructions

Ælohîm

Universal Mind moving away from the centre following instructions

Sphere of Activity

Circumferential Extent

Figure 22.1 above depicts the two opposed movements of the universal mind, concentric and eccentric. The concentric movement shows the universal mind moving toward Ælohîm (the center) to receive commandments, and the eccentric movement shows the universal mind moving away from Ælohîm, following commandments to manifest every evident, demonstrable, and determined moral existence in its sphere of activity. These opposed movements give direction to life and vital movement to the assimilated, reflective, transient life. The Hebrew text conveys that Henoch, the "moral sense," is necessary in transient life for the upward-progressing life movement of the soul. The progressing upward movement of the soul is also conveyed by the Hebrew words *Æth-Ælohîm* given in this verse.

GENERATION OF HENOCH SIMILITUDES

The Hebrew word *âhoreî* reveals that by centralizing elements (electrons, protons, and other constituent parts) Henoch's similitudes began to be shaped. Centralization confined the elements from free movement. It gave them a definite form or expression that resulted in an effluvium or ethereal, spirituous emanation of Henoch's similitudes. In succession, the effluvium was passed from one state of development to another in a rectilinear movement that made evident the similitudes' potential life or power of being.

The Hebrew word *hôlid* reveals that their potential life was made evident as the universal mind passed the effluvium from one nature to another in an eccentric movement designed to extend, rise, and unfold the effluvium in all directions within its sphere of activity. This conveys an execution of power over the universal quaternary and over Methoûshalah enabling the universal mind to extend, rise, and unfold the effluvium throughout the circumferential extent. The details of this event are disclosed in the underlying meaning of the number 300 given in this verse.

UNDERLYING MEANING OF THE NUMBER 300

The Hebrew names *shelosh* and *mæoth* make up the number 300.

Shelosh reveals that the universal mind went a great distance, across the circumferential extent, to the farthest side of the boundary to give vital movement to matter and to unite en masse, fashion, and place the different qualities of Henoch (represented by the effluvium) into it. *Mæôth* reveals that this was a transitional movement that led the universal mind to mutate. That is to say, as the universal mind endeavored to unfold the effluvium, it underwent changes in its nature, essence, qualities, and attributes, and it altered in form.

Accordingly, these changes signaled Henoch's similitudes being brought forth relative to the diverse mutations of the universal mind.

The Hebrew words *iôled banîm w-banôth* reveal that the universal mind emanated many offspring resembling its faculty Henoch. These emanations were intelligible embodiments characterizing Henoch's circumscriptive extent. They were the selfsameness of Henoch produced to provide the souls of men corporate force and panging qualities (moral precepts) vital to the souls' spiritual unfoldment. That is to say, possessing the faculty Henoch enabled the universal mind to instill the precepts of God in the myriad of souls that would eventually become humanity.

SUMMARY

Genesis 5:22 reveals that the phrase "walked with God" literally signifies "to be carried in every sense, and to go to and to come." This phrase conveys the idea that the faculty Henoch enabled the universal mind to follow the commandments set by the Ælohîm (the unity of the Gods). It reveals that the commandments were intended as authoritative rules of action applied particularly to commands respecting moral conduct. As precepts of God, moral sense was instilled in the myriad of souls that would eventually become humanity. It reveals that Henoch, the moral sense, is necessary in transient life for the upward-progressing life movement of the souls.

★ PRACTICAL APPLICATION

Genesis 5:22 reveals that moral precepts are vital to the soul's spiritual unfoldment. Further, it reveals commandments are considered authoritative rules of action applicable to commands respecting moral conduct. Commandments are relevant to man's conduct as a social being and to right and wrongdoing. Following established principles (moral precepts) binds us, as moral agents, to performing social duties supported by evidence of reason. Society enables us to conform to rules of right or to accept rules respecting social duties. Good examples of moral conduct include developing virtuosity, being just, and being irreproachable in one's sexual relations. Principles and practices in regard to right, wrong, and duty are essential in building a good moral sense, which is vital to our spiritual unfoldment.

CRITICAL THINKING

1. What is the meaning of the phrase "walked with God?"
2. The phrase "walked with God" enabled the universal mind to follow the _____ set by the Ælohîm.
3. The commandments are intended as _____ _____ of _____.
4. The commandments were applied particularly to commands respecting _____ _____, _____, _____, _____, and _____
5. For what purpose were the similitudes of Henoch created?
6. What is the literal meaning of the Hebrew name Ælohîm?
7. Why is the faculty Henoch necessary in the life of the soul?

(Answers in Appendix B)

[1.] Refer to the meaning of *Ælohîm* in footnote 3 of chapter 1.

[2.] *The Center* refers to Ælohîm as the directing power laying down the host of moral laws enabling the universal mind to unfold every demonstrable and determined moral existence within its sphere of activity, the circumference.

23

SIMILITUDES OF HENOCH, PART 2

GENESIS 5:23

- Translation from the King James Version of the Bible: "And all the days of Enoch were three hundred sixty and five years."
- The literal English translation as it appears in *The Hebraic Tongue Restored*: "And they were, all the days (manifested lights) of Henoch, five and six-tens of revolving change and three hundreds of revolution."
- Transliteration from *The Hebraic Tongue Restored*: "Wa-îhîou chol îmeî Hanôch hamesh w-shishîm shanah w-shelosh mæôth shanah."

  The following interpretation of Genesis 5:23 is spiritual in nature, not physical.

PROEM

Genesis 5:23 sums up the development of Henoch's similitudes and the successive change that took place in the universal mind.

The transliterated Hebrew words *îhîou chol îmeî Hanôch* reveal how Henoch's similitudes were arranged, prepared, and given agreeable forms during their luminous period of manifestation[1], and how it involved advancing all movements of the creative waters

183

to render the necessary elements to build the similitudes. The underlying meaning of the number 365 given in this verse conveys the particulars.

UNDERLYING MEANING OF THE NUMBER 365

The Hebrew names *hamesh*, *shishîm*, *shelosh*, and *mæôth* compose the number 365. Each one of these names requires examination to unveil the meaning of this number.

Hamesh (number five) reveals the great effort exerted upon elementary existence (the creative waters) to manifest elements, to make them palpable and compact, and subsequently, to enable the universal mind to extract them from their depth.

Hamesh tells us that upon extracting the elements, the passive and conditional casuality of the universal mind took place. It conveys that being in contact with the elements produced impressions enabling the universal mind to fashion the elements accordingly. This rendered Henoch's similitudes evident.

Shishîm (number sixty) makes known that the similitudes were bestowed with the following:

- proportion in regard to the arrangement of their constituent parts
- measure (precision)
- harmony (symmetry)
- equality (uniformity)
- equilibrium (balance)
- parallelism (resembling each other)
- fitness or adaptability to develop universally

UNIVERSAL DEVELOPMENT OF HENOCH'S SIMILITUDES

Shelosh (number three) reveals that Henoch's similitudes were developed across the circumferential extent and that the qualities of the similitudes (and their various aspects) were involved in matter, which influenced them to develop universally.

Mæôth and *shanah* communicate that these were transitional movements that led the universal mind to mutate repeatedly and relocated it to its state of seity, the state at which it had begun to move. However, the universal mind was not found, at the end of this period of activity, in the same state that it was when it emanated Henoch. It connotes the universal mind had become more knowledgeable from having reproduced and developed its corporate force and panging qualities (chapter 22), and from having produced its "eager shaft of death," Methoûshalah (chapter 21).

SUMMARY

Genesis 5:23 reiterates how Henoch's similitudes were developed and the successive change that took place in the universal mind after this period of activity.

★ PRACTICAL APPLICATION

To this point, we have learned that Genesis 5 is about the universal mind developing its faculties and about building man in its image. As an image of the universal mind, man is endowed with like faculties, and these are to be developed during the evolutionary processes of his soul. Just as the universal mind developed its faculties, so man, whose image resembles the universal mind, must develop his latent faculties.

The process of evolution accomplishes this, but we cannot have evolution without having something to evolve. Evolution does not create anything; it only reveals it. What we are today is the partial unfolding of our faculties. Therefore, we must endeavor to manifest them in substance. Form will be the expression resulting from consciously directing our intelligence to continue to experience the progression of our evolving powers in matter.

Our goal is to "go home," as it were, and get back to God, carrying with us the fruitage (mental products, results of experiences, studies, and development) of our brief sojourn in the foreign land of the physical world.

CRITICAL THINKING

1. Genesis 5:23 reveals that the universal mind exerted great effort upon the creative waters to manifest something. What did the universal mind desire to manifest?

2. Developing Henoch's similitudes was a transition that effected a successive change in the universal mind. What happened to the universal mind with this change?

(Answers in Appendix B)

[1.] See the generation of Henoch's similitudes in Genesis 5:22.

24

GOD TOOK HENOCH

GENESIS 5:24

- Translation from the King James Version of the Bible: "And Enoch walked with God: and he was not, for God took him."
- The literal English translation as it appears in *The Hebraic Tongue Restored*: "And he applied himself to tread, Henoch (in the steps) of HIM, the Gods, and nought (no substance) of him; for he resumed him, HE-the Being of beings."
- Transliteration from *The Hebraic Tongue Restored*: "Wa-îthehallech Hanôch æth-ha-Ælohîm w'æine-nou chi-lakah âoth-ô Ælohîm."

The following interpretation of Genesis 5:24 is spiritual in nature, not physical.

PROEM

In chapter 18, we learned that the universal mind emanated its central might and panging qualities, which Moses named *Henoch*. In chapter 22 we were told that the universal mind made similitudes of Henoch for the benefit of mankind—that is, to instill the precepts of God in the myriad of souls that would eventually become humanity. In this chapter, the sagacious examinations of Ælohîm upon Henoch are made known.

The Hebrew words *chi-lakah âoth-ô Ælohîm* express that Ælohîm assimilated Henoch (converted to a like substance) and seized its identity, anticipating with pleasure having its spirit, which He scrutinized (observed, examined, or investigated closely) and then put back (resumed) into the universal mind. That is to say, Ælohîm (He, the unity of the Gods) seized the spirit of Henoch to scrutinize or observe closely the temper (disposition), character, nature, or tendency of this faculty, whether intellectual, moral, or emotional. In other words, Ælohîm took possession of this faculty to examine its quintessence: its vital or essential parts, qualities, and virtues; its pure and concentrated essence; and its purest or highest state of existing. Afterward, Genesis 5:24 reveals that Henoch was returned (resumed) into Adam, the universal mind. It further reveals that Ælohîm took no substance of Henoch, for Henoch had transmuted in its mode of existence. Henoch became insubstantial. This does not mean that Henoch became unreal. Rather, it became an abstraction, good or evil, of spirituality.

HENOCH, A VITAL POWER

The Hebrew word *æine-nou*[1] reveals that: "no substance of Henoch ceased to exist without Henoch ceasing to be, for Ælohîm withdrew this faculty unto himself" (Cosmogony of Moses, THTR, 327). The Hebrew text discloses that the Hebrew root *aon* (part of the word *æine*) develops ideas most opposed in appearance, such as "being and nothingness," "strength and weakness," etc. But here, this peculiarity rests less in the root itself than in the object to which it is opposed. Whatever is admitted as existing—good or evil, strong or weak—this root manifested by the adverbial relation *ain* will be its absolute opposite. If the substance is granted as "all," *ain* is the symbol of "nothing." If the substance is considered as "nothing," *ain* is the symbol of "all."

The Hebrew text also discloses that *ain* characterizes the absence of substance and of all reality. It is an abstraction, good or evil, of spirituality. The text further makes known that this is the origin of the syllable *in*, used sometimes to change the signification of words.

In the case referred to, the adverbial relation of *ain* indicates a transmutation in the mode of existence of Henoch. It is not a simple change of place or removal as the translators of the Bible understand it. If Henoch was substance, it ceased being this and became spirit—vital power. The Hebrew text reveals that Henoch was "in him," or insubstantial.

SUMMARY

Genesis 5:24 reveals that Ælohîm seized the spirit of Henoch to scrutinize the temper, character, and nature of this faculty, whether intellectual, moral, or emotional. Further, it reveals that Ælohîm resumed Henoch into the universal mind (Adam), and that Ælohîm took no substance of Henoch because Henoch had transmuted in its mode of existence. Henoch became insubstantial, a spiritual abstraction of good or evil.

★ *PRACTICAL APPLICATION*

Like all the other faculties of the universal mind, the essence of Henoch is endowed to each human soul. This tells us that our Higher Self is furnished with the highest essence of power, the highest qualities and virtues, and the purest and most concentrated essence (Henoch's quintessence). Hence, developing this faculty will enable us to tread in accordance with the precepts set by Ælohîm respecting moral conduct, laws, instructions, injunctions, and maxims (chief premises or established principles).

Further, we learned that following the precepts set by Ælohîm will give vital movement to our existence while transiting the material world, and it will facilitate the upward movement of our soul through evolution.

Evolution raises the level of our awareness into supra-mental realms, eventually flowing into still higher levels as the seed develops into a plant. We then pass from purely physical consciousness through emotion and mind consciousness into the region of the Higher Self, which is beyond and above them. The physical nature is then spiritualized, and the personality and the Higher Self are combined in pursuit of the Ideal. The fruits gained in the pursuit of the Ideal are the result of bodily life, bodily resistance, and bodily effort, from which the experience and ultimate transmutation of the soul grows in spiritual stature, richness, beauty, and light.

CRITICAL THINKING

1. Genesis 5:24 reveals that Ælohîm seized the spirit of Henoch. For what reason?
2. Why didn't Ælohîm take any substance of Henoch?
3. Henoch ceased being substance and became spirit or _____ _____.

(Answers in Appendix B)

[1.] Fabre d'Olivet states that "at the very time of the Samaritan version of the Bible, the most ancient of all, and shortly after the captivity of Babylon, this expression so vital, *æine-nou*, was not understood. The author of the Samaritan version substituted for the Hebrew *æine-nou* the words 'and-no-sign-of-him,'" adding, "for-they-carried-him away, the angels." "The Chaldaic uses the same words 'and-no-sign-of-him.' The Hellenists take a turn still more curious: 'And he was not found.'" And Saint Jerome (creator of the Latin Vulgate version of the Bible) takes a middle course in saying, "And he appeared not."

25

THE TIE OF WHAT TENDS TO DISSOLUTION: LAMECH

GENESIS 5:25

- Translation from the King James Version of the Bible: "And Methuselah lived an hundred eighty and seven years and begat Lamech."
- The literal English translation as it appears in *The Hebraic Tongue Restored*: "And he was in being, Methushalah, seven and eight tens of revolving change, and one hundred of revolution and he begat Lamech, the tie of dissolution."
- Transliteration from *The Hebraic Tongue Restored*: "Wa îhî Methoûshelah shebah w-shemonîm shanah w'mâth shanah wa-îôled æth-Lamech."

The following interpretation of Genesis 5:25 is spiritual in nature, not physical.

PROEM

This chapter discloses a new period of activity began for the universal mind. Based on what we learned from previous chapters, this means that a new faculty is due to come forth. The best way to describe the power of this new faculty is by explaining what it does and its mode of existence.

Genesis 5:25 reveals that this faculty keeps the memory of past events from dissolving, after the soul passes through transition (the commonly known death of the physical body). Further, it makes known that the faculty Methoûshalah (the "eager shaft of death") enabled the universal mind to bring forth the new faculty, which Moses named *Lamech*.

Lamech is the tie of what tends to dissolution, the pliant bond of things. It chains human existences in sequence and keeps the memory of each incarnation together in the subconscious mind—that part of the mind that conceives all mental processes without any conscious apprehension of their occurrence.

The transliterated Hebrew word *îhî* discloses how the elements to form this new faculty were rendered manifest and obvious in response to the impulsions of the universal mind upon elementary existence (the creative waters). *Îhî* and the Hebrew name *Methoûshalah* reveal that the manifestation of these elements enabled the universal mind to become conscious of its ability to extend, rise, and unfold the elements into the qualities of its forthcoming faculty. The underlying meaning of the number 187 given in this verse offers additional details.

UNDERLYING MEANING OF THE NUMBER 187

The Hebrew names *shebah*, *shemonîm*, and *mâth* compose the number 187. Their individual examination is critical in order to render their meaning accurately.

Shebah (number seven) reveals that the universal mind fructified the qualities of its new faculty and subsequently endeavored to involve them into matter. It necessitated precipitating or rushing the qualities with steep descent into matter. These were harsh, rigorous, exacting, inordinate, and vehement movements of the universal mind upon material substance. Consequently, the qualities were animated upon entering matter.

Shemonim (number eighty) discloses that involving the qualities into matter was a process whereby the universal mind descended onto its sphere of activity to mobilize (stir) the creative waters in order to draw elements that subsequently were rendered into an image or resemblance of its new faculty in material substance.

Math (number one hundred) reveals that the task of extending, dilating, and manifesting the faculty exteriorly was in sympathy with divine laws and they were transitional movements that led the universal mind to mutate repeatedly.

Accordingly, mutations caused changes in the nature, essence, qualities, and attributes of the universal mind. It altered it in form, enabling it to emanate its new faculty, either in the order of things, or in the order of time, relative to its diverse mutations. This knowledge was unveiled from the Hebrew word *shanah*.

THE BIRTH OF LAMECH

The Hebrew words *îôled æth-Lamech* make known that the new faculty was brought forth and that it was named Lamech.

The Hebrew text explains that this Lamech differs from the Lamech in Genesis 4:18 (not covered in this book). The latter Lamech is the descendant of the universal mind (Adam) by Sheth. It differs from the former Lamech only by the generation to which it belongs. The latter Lamech has the same character but in another nature. The former, which issued from the generation of Kain, is the sixth descendant from the universal mind; the latter, which belongs to that of Sheth, is the eighth. The former has two corporeal wives—that is, two physical faculties—that gave it three sons, or rather three cosmogonic principles:

- the source of all fertility (Jabal, Gen. 4:20)
- the source of all prosperity (Jubal, Gen. 4:21)
- the source of all power upon the Earth (Thubal-Kain, Gen. 4:22)

The latter left only one son, Noah (a cosmogonic principle). Noah enabled the universal mind to see mankind finish and begin again (refer to the meaning of *Noah* in chapter 28). Let us now return to Lamech, the descendant of the universal mind by Sheth.

The roots of the name *Lamech* are clear and simple. These roots are *lou*, which contains all ideas of cohesion, agglutination, or being united by a tenacious substance, and *mouch*, which develops the ideas of liquefaction, dissolution, prostration, submission, etc. Hence, Lamech is the faculty that "ties" that which tends to dissolution and prevents it from being dissolved. That is, Lamech is "the knot" that arrests dissolution and is the "the pliant bond of things."

In his book *The Unknown God*, F. J. Mayers states that Lamech is "the chain or sequence of human existences." This conveys that Lamech is the pliant bond that fastens each incarnation of the soul like a chain. Lamech is the "tie" of each incarnation kept together. It is the faculty of the mind by which it retains the knowledge of past events, ideas, or impressions. Lamech keeps them from being dissolved. It enables man to remember or recollect things that continue to exist in the mind exempted from oblivion. Hence, Lamech is the power by which the mind reproduces past impressions by remembering. Remembering exercises that power when things occur spontaneously to man's thoughts. For instance, in *recollection* we make a distinct effort to collect again or to call back what we know has been formerly in our mind. This is different from *reminiscence*, which is an intermediate state between remembrance and recollection where we are conscious of a process of recalling past occurrences—without the distinct reference to particular things, which characterizes *recollection.*

Lamech dwells in the subconscious. There, it arrests dissolution of all life experiences or events that are received throughout the many incarnations.

SEQUENCE OF HUMAN EXISTENCES

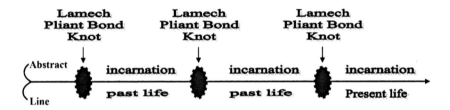

Figure 25.1 above depicts how the souls' existences are chained to form a continuous lifeline. It depicts Lamech as the *sequence of human existences,* as a *pliant bond* and as a *knot* fastening each incarnation.

As the pliant bond, Lamech binds each incarnation of the soul as a cord, a chain, or a rope to hold the memory of passed lives together. It unites, links, or connects past events that can be easily bent (or forgotten) and readily yield to force (at transition of the soul) without breaking (or cessation of remembrance).

Lamech characterizes the kind of bond that prevents a life—at first vehement and violent, and now subdued, softened, cast down, and ready to be dissolved (at death)—from being dissolved and from being wholly dissipated; it goes into the subconscious. This is the bond of association (or union) arresting dissolution of each incarnation.

As the knot, Lamech is the abstract line conceived to be going from one point to another (or one life to another), adhering and uniting successive incarnations of the soul by mutual ties (knots), a sympathetic movement, which joins and serves as liaison to unite each past life in the subconscious.

HIEROGLYPHIC MEANING OF THE NAME *LAMECH*

Lamech represents a movement without term, an action whose duration is limitless. It is an indefinite expansion directed toward the universalization of a people, a considerable number of men (minds) united by a common bond (the universal mind). Lamech enables the universal mind to make the assemblage of all minds all-embracing, all-reaching, pervading all.

Further, Lamech enables the universal mind to attenuate (make submissive) the assimilated, reflective, and transient (terrestrial) life. This is the preceding step to manifesting the radiant movement or objectivity of existence proper in equilibrium. We shall see in a later chapter that Lamech enables the universal mind to bring forth the equilibratory force or directing energy that enables the universal mind to unfold the homogeneous ground (the "adamah") from which the material world proceeds.

ADAM'S MICROCOSM (9/10)

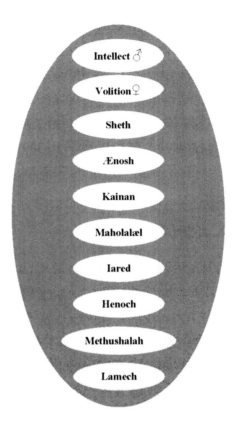

Figure 25.2 above depicts the addition of Lamech to the unfolding microcosm of the universal mind (Adam). The growing faculties of the universal mind are now composed of intellect (male principle), volition/will (female principle), Sheth (Adam's power to frame the foundation of the soul), Ænosh (Adam's physical faculties, corporeal man), Kainan (Adam's general invading force), Maholalæl (Adam's rising might and brightness), Iared (Adam's powers of steadfastness and perseverance), Henoch (Adam's corporate force and panging qualities), Methoûshalah (Adam's "eager shaft of death), and Lamech (Adam's ability to tie what tends to dissolution).

SUMMARY

Genesis 5:25 reveals that the universal mind emanated a new faculty (Lamech) to keep the memory of past events from dissolving after the soul passes through transition, or the so-called death. It reveals that this faculty represents a movement without term and is directed toward the universalization of a considerable number of men (minds). Moreover, it reveals that this faculty enables the universal mind to attenuate the assimilated, reflective, and transient life.

★ *PRACTICAL APPLICATION*

Genesis 5:25 reveals how each incarnation of the soul is fastened as a chain and how this fastening holds the memory of past lives together. An example of how memory continues to exist after transition of the soul is found in the power to remember friends from past lives. According to ancient philosophies, when we recognize people we think we've never met before or it seems as though we have always known them, these are actually friends from previous incarnations. There is an immediate, sympathetic response at first meeting. When this happens, we must make every effort to rediscover them through familiar physical, mental, and spiritual qualities. Friends from previous incarnations are usually very near us. They are drawn into the orbit of our life by the friendship born in the dim, distant past. The immediate attraction we feel to the inner and outer features of an individual are our first indication that we have found a friend of the past. Such a friend is drawn to us by a prenatal sense of friendship.

CRITICAL THINKING

1. Genesis 5:25 reveals that the universal mind emanated a new faculty to keep the memory of past events from dissolving after souls pass through transition. What is the name of this faculty?

2. The faculty Lamech is described in two different modes. Describe the modes.

3. Hieroglyphically, Lamech represents a movement without term, an action whose duration is limitless and is directed toward the universalization of a people. Briefly, describe what this means.

(Answers in Appendix B)

26

THE EAGER SHAFT OF DEATH: SIMILITUDES OF METHOÛSHALAH, PART 1

GENESIS 5:26

- Translation from the King James Version of the Bible: "And Methuselah lived after he begat Lamech seven hundred eighty and two years and begat sons and daughters."
- The literal English translation as it appears in *The Hebraic Tongue Restored*: "And he lived, Methushalah after the causing him to beget that same Lamech, two and eight tens of revolving change, and seven hundreds of revolution and he begat sons and daughters (many issued offspring)."
- Transliteration from *The Hebraic Tongue Restored*: "Wa îhî Methoûshelah âhoreî hôlid-ô æth Lamech, shethaîm w-shemonîm shanah, w-shebah mæôth shanah wa-îôled banîm w-banôth."

The following interpretation of Genesis 5:26 is spiritual in nature, not physical.

PROEM

In this chapter, the production of Methoûshalah's similitudes is made known. Methoûshalah, you may recall, represents the "eager shaft of death" (refer to chapter 21), a faculty that will enable the soul to swiftly hurtle to the tranquil and happy existence after passing through transition, or the so-called death. Like a blueprint from which specimens are modeled, Methoûshalah's similitudes will have the same ability genealogically. Genesis 5:26 reveals the intricacy of steps taken to develop the symbolical sons and daughters of Methuselah—its similitudes.

SUBSTANTIALIZING METHOÛSHALAH'S SIMILITUDES

The Hebrew word *îhî* reveals that elementary existence manifested elements in response to the universal mind's impulsions upon it. The manifestation of these elements enabled the universal mind to become conscious of conditions pertaining to its faculty Methoûshalah and its ability to generate the souls' power to hurtle swiftly toward the eternity of existence upon transition.

All notions attached to Methoûshalah's identity being transferred into the elements to render its similitudes in substance are revealed in the Hebrew words *âhoreî* and *hôlid* and in the number 782.

Âhoreî furnishes the idea of compressing and confining the elements from free movement in order to set and give them a definite, compact, centralized form or expression consistent with an ethereal spiritual emanation of the similitudes. In succession, the emanations were made to pass from one state to another in a rectilinear movement that made visible the similitudes' potential life or power of being.

Hôlid reveals that their power of being was made evident as the universal mind passed the emanations from one nature to another in an eccentric movement designed to extend, rise, and unfold the emanations in all directions within its creative area of activity. Moreover, it reveals that this movement expanded the intellectual powers of the universal mind. This enabled the universal mind to understand how to keep the emanations from dissolving necessitating activating the universal quaternary and its faculty Lamech to keep the emanations intact. Their evolution is revealed in the interpretation of the number 782 given in this verse.

UNDERLYING MEANING OF THE NUMBER 782

The Hebrew names *shethaîm, shemonîm, shebah,* and *mæôth* compose the number 782, and they are interpreted separately to unveil the underlying meaning of this number.

Shethaîm (number two) contains all ideas of passing from one state to another. It reveals that the spiritual emanations of the similitudes had passed from their effluvium state into another form of expression.

Shemonim (number eighty) conveys that their new form of expression was accomplished as the emanations were spread across the entire sphere of activity (the circumferential extent) and were made to render images, representations, or similitudes of Methoûshalah in material substance. This means Methoûshalah's similitudes were given separate and distinct existence. It was a universalization of the similitudes infinitely succeeding one another, though not yet perfected.

The Hebrew word *shanah* reveals that the similitudes mutated repeatedly as they passed from one state of development to another— the process of gradual evolution from a previous stage to that in which the original idea was fully exhibited.

MANIFESTATION OF METHOÛSHALAH'S SIMILITUDES

Shebah (number seven) contains all ideas of accomplishment, of consummation of things. It conveys that the universal mind finished what it intended: to build Methoûshalah's similitudes.

Mæoth reveals that the similitudes were made to develop to the extent of Methoûshalah's circumscription. Further, it makes known that the desire to extend, dilate, and manifest the similitudes exteriorly was a sympathetic and reciprocal movement in accord with divine laws, and it was a transition that led the universal mind to mutate repeatedly. *Shanah* discloses that mutations in turn caused changes in the nature, essence, qualities, and attributes of the universal mind, and that it altered it in form enabling it to bring forth Methoûshalah's similitudes, either in the order of things, or in the order of time, relative to its diverse mutations.

The Hebrew words *iôled banîm w-banôth* tells us that the universal mind emanated many issued offspring resembling Methoûshalah. In other words, as the universal mind passed from one state of being to another (the result of mutations), generative extensions—the symbolical sons and daughters—were developed. They were intelligible embodiments characterizing Methoûshalah's circumscriptive extent. They were the essence of Methoûshalah, created to provide the souls of men with the ability to swiftly hurtle upward toward the eternity of existence upon transition.

SUMMARY

Genesis 5:26 reveals that the universal mind produced similitudes of its faculty Methoûshalah to endow the souls of men with the power to swiftly hurtle toward the eternity of existence upon transition.

★ PRACTICAL APPLICATION

Chapter 21 revealed that Moses acknowledged two kinds of deaths: Methoûshalah (the "eager shaft of death," which swiftly hurls souls toward the eternity of existence) and Methoushael (the gulf or abyss of death, which precipitates, hastens without preparation, or throws headlong from a height while devouring, destroying, and consuming wantonly and with violence). I think we all agree that Methoûshalah is the preferred method of departing from this world.

The soul's evil conduct while incarnated can keep that soul from swiftly hurtling toward the eternity of existence upon transition. This kind of conduct is characterized by wickedness, a depraved or corrupt disposition or heart, evil practices, sinfulness, vice, immorality, crime, opposition to goodness, viciousness, iniquitousness—all of which violate the law of right between man and man—and nefariousness, which violates the most sacred obligations. All are deserving of punishment.

Upon transition, such wicked souls, we are told, are precipitated downward to the fathomless pit. They are thrown headlong into an open gulf, where they are consumed wantonly and with violence. This conforms to Proverbs 2:22 and Deuteronomy 30:16–18 of the Bible. Proverbs 2:22 states, "For the wicked shall be cut off from the earth, and the transgressor shall be rooted out of it." Deuteronomy 30:16–18 state that the Lord denounces those who turn away and will not walk in his ways, and he advises them that they will perish.

On the other hand, upon transition, souls that tried to live in harmony with cosmic purpose or divine laws are swiftly hurled upward into the tranquil and happy, in good order and in the way of salvation or preservation from destruction. An allowance is made for those who did not make the mark but who repented or felt contrition (inherent in all human beings) for wrongdoing. They are exonerated and granted salvation, delivered and preserved from destruction.

CRITICAL THINKING

1. Genesis 5:26 reveals that the universal mind generated similitudes of its faculty Methoûshalah. For what purpose were these similitudes developed?

(Answer in Appendix B)

27

THE EAGER SHAFT OF DEATH: SIMILITUDES OF METHOÛSHALAH, PART 2

GENESIS 5:27

- Translation from the King James Version of the Bible: "And all the days of Methuselah were nine hundred sixty and nine years: and he died."
- The literal English translation as it appears in *The Hebraic Tongue Restored*: "And they were, all the days (manifested lights) of Methushalah, nine and six tens of revolving change, and nine hundreds of revolution: and he ceased (to be in being)."
- Transliteration from *The Hebraic Tongue Restored*: "Wa îhîou chol-îemeî Methoûshelah theshah w-shishîm shanah, w-theshah mæoth shanah; wa-îamôth."

The following interpretation of Genesis 5:27 is spiritual in nature, not physical.

PROEM

Following the emanation of Methoûshalah's similitudes (chapter 26), their progression into a consolidated state is next. The underlying

205

meaning of the number 969 given in Genesis 5:27 conveys their gradual transformation, which hastened their advancement. Further, Genesis 5:27 conveys the revolving changes undergone by the universal mind and the completion of a period of activities.

UNDERLYING MEANING OF THE NUMBER 969

The Hebrew names *theshah*, *shishîm*, *theshah*, and *mæoth* compose the number 969. Their individual interpretation unveils the following information.

Theshah (number nine) reveals that Methoûshalah's similitudes were gradually transformed (metamorphosed) into a consolidated state to preserve them from loss and to keep them in an entire state. By degrees the universal mind molded and carefully closed the similitudes' animated matter. This quickening effect resulted upon consolidation of Methoûshalah's constituent parts. It conveys consolidation cemented, guaranteed, and plastered the similitudes.

Subsequently, a real and evident existence became obvious. *Shishîm* (number sixty) reveals that the similitudes were manifested in substance. They were given proportion, measure, harmony, equality, equilibrium, parallelism, and fitness. This means Methoûshalah's similitudes were sized, arranged, and given dimensions, which reduced them to precision. They were adapted to one another to form a connected whole. They were given uniformity—that is, likeness in magnitude, value, degree, and the like. They were evenly balanced in order to preserve their equilibrium, and they were adapted to swiftly hurl the souls of men to the eternity of existence upon transition, just like the original pattern from which they were modeled; that is, they were given the likeness in nature, qualities, and appearance as Methoûshalah, the universal mind's "eager shaft of death."

Shanah discloses that universal and ontological mutations went hand-in-hand with the similitudes appearing in substance. *Theshah* reveals that their boundaries, designations, and definitions were affected as they passed from one state of development to another evolving into precise forms. This completed a period of activity for the universal mind and a transition took place. This was a transmutation that befell upon the universal mind following the Law of Cause and Effect. *Mæôth* and *shanah* concur.

TRANSMUTATION OF THE UNIVERSAL MIND

Shanah discloses that the transmutation was cyclic in nature and revolved around the recent period of activities. Once it ended, the universal mind returned to its state of seity from whence it had begun to move. *Shanah* makes known that the universal mind was not found at the end of this period of activity in the same state that it was at its beginning. The Hebrew word *îamôth* informs us that the universal mind had transmuted to a different way of being. This was a successive change under natural laws (cause and effect) that transformed that universal mind upon effecting the purpose for which Methoûshalah's similitudes were created—namely, to endow the souls of men with an inherent transitional movement that would activate upon transition and swiftly hurl them to a different way of existence.

SUMMARY

Genesis 5:27 reveals that Methoûshalah's similitudes progressed into a consolidated state, which hastened their advancement. Further, it conveys that the universal mind was transformed into a different way of being upon finishing this period of activity, a successive change that came under the Law of Cause and Effect.

★ *PRACTICAL APPLICATION*

Chapter 5 of the Genesis account reveals that the universal mind always exerts great effort in developing its faculties and their similitudes. First, it causes elementary life to produce the elements necessary to build its faculties and their similitudes. Then, it quickens the similitudes after transforming them into a consolidated state. This scenario demonstrates that effort always precedes attainment, and the concept is applicable to all human affairs.

In all human activities, "there are efforts, and there are results, and the strength of the effort is the measure of the result. Gifts, powers, material, intellectual, and spiritual possessions are the fruits of effort; they are thoughts completed, objects accomplished, visions realized."[1] Attainments do not happen by chance. We must voluntarily encounter the vicissitudes of life in order to profit from our experience. "We must make sacrifices, put forth undaunted effort, exercise great faith in order to overcome the apparent insurmountable and realize the vision of our heart. We must go through darkness and heartache to see the light and receive the joy. We must go through long and arduous journeys to behold the pleasant goal."[2] There is always effort behind results.

CRITICAL THINKING

1. Genesis 5:27 addresses the transformation of Methoûshalah's similitudes. This is an indication that the similitudes were _____, which resulted in an _____ _____.

2. The universal mind transformed into a different way of being after giving reality to the similitudes of Methoûshalah. This change came as a result of a law. What is the name of this law?

(Answers in Appendix B)

---

[1] James Allen, *As a Man Thinketh*, 82.

[2] Ibid.

28

THE REPOSE OF NATURE: NOAH

GENESIS 5:28–29

- Translation from the King James Version of the Bible: "And Lamech lived an hundred eighty and two years, and begat a son" (Gen. 5:28). "And he called his name Noah, saying, this same shall comfort us concerning our work and toil of our hands because of the ground, which the Lord hath cursed" (Gen. 5:29).

- The literal English translation as it appears in *The Hebraic Tongue Restored*: "And he lived, Lamech, two and eight tens of revolving change, and one hundred of revolution: and he begat a son, an issued offspring" (Gen. 5:28). "And he assigned for name to him, Noah, thus declaring his thought: this will release us (will lessen, relieve us) from the hard working our, and from the great natural hindrance of the hands ours, because of the adamic (elementary ground) which he has cursed it, IHOAH" (Gen. 5:29).

- Transliteration from *The Hebraic Tongue Restored*: "Wa îhî Lamech shethîm w-shemonîm shanah w-mâth shanah: wa-îôled ben" (Gen. 5:28). "Wa-îkkerâ æth-sham-ô Noah l'æmor zeh înahome-nou mi-mahoshenou, w-me-whitzebôn îadeînou min-ha-âdamah âsher ærorha IHOAH" (Gen. 5:29).

210

The following interpretation of Genesis 5:28–29 are spiritual in nature, not physical.

PROEM

Genesis 5:28–29 reveals that the universal mind brought forth a new faculty, an extension of itself whose activity is to clothe or cover all of its other faculties with a physical vehicle of consciousness or "ark." This is a long-continued process of evolution by which the three lower kingdoms of nature (mineral, plant, and animal) will become established on earth.

The Hebrew word *îhî* reveals that the universal mind began the process of developing its new faculty—first, by extracting elements (electrons, protons, and other constituent ingredients) from elementary existence, second, by utilizing its faculty Lamech to enable it to keep the elements bound in union, and third, by proceeding to develop the elements into the new faculty. Concealed under the number 182 given in Genesis 5:28 is the knowledge of this event.

UNDERLYING MEANING OF THE NUMBER 182

To discover the real significance of the number 182, we will examine the Hebrew names that compose this number: *shethîm, shemonîm,* and *mâth.*

Shethîm (number two) discloses a passage from one state to another, and *shemonîm* (number eighty) is the action of accumulating forms. Therefore, *shethîm shemonîm* (number 82) reveals that the manifested elements were passed from elementary existence to the circumferential extent (the entire sphere of activity), where the universal mind exerted its powers to produce its offspring—that is, to produce the continuity of an existence by generation.

Exerting power over the elements resulted in altering their form, state, quality, or essence. The Hebrew word *shanah* reveals that the elements mutated repeatedly as they were passed from one state to another conveying the developmental stages of the offspring.

Mâth (number one hundred) reveals that the offspring developed to the extent of Lamech's circumscription—till this point, this is as far as the universal mind had developed—and that developing the offspring was a sympathetic and reciprocal movement in harmony and accord with divine laws. It was a transitional step that led the universal mind to mutate; consequently, it changed its nature, essence, qualities, and attributes and it altered it in form thereby enabling it to bring forth its offspring.

A NEW PROGENY IS BORN

The Hebrew words *iôled ben* confirm that the universal mind generated an extension of itself. Generating this extension was an active production proceeding from potentiality in action. That is to say, the universal mind exercised its conceptive, intellectual faculty to produce an emanation that was intelligible and sentient (capable of perceiving).

Literally, the universal mind produced:

- a formation (It caused the emanation to exist.)
- an embodiment (It produced an organized body.)
- a construction (It made a fabrication.)

The Hebrew verb *nahome* communicates the meaning that Moses wished to give to the distinguishing qualities of this extension—namely, "to support," "to moderate," "to temper." This conveys that this new faculty enables the universal mind to:

- carry or bring subsistence (real being, actual existence) into matter;
- keep subsistence within reasonable bounds;
- preside over subsistence; and
- regulate or bring subsistence to a moderate state—that is, to bring actual existence to a proper degree of hardness by heating and cooling.

ASSIGNING A NAME TO THE NEW OFFSPRING

Genesis 5:29 reveals that the universal mind gave a name to its extension. When carefully examining the Hebrew verb *îkkerâ*, which was translated as "called" by the Bible translators, we find many significations springing from its Hebrew root "*kr*," which literally signifies a "character," a "characteristic sign," or an "engraving." It contains the ideas of being incisive, penetrating, ingrained, or engraved; of being any character, letter, or writing; or of being an inscription, memorial, or carving.

It acquires the meaning of "call" from its definitions: "to cry out, to scream; to call anyone's attention; to hail anyone; to designate a thing by name; to name anyone; to evoke or convocate." It can also mean "an incision or cutting in, the action of digging, and a ditch or an abyss."

By studying these various significations, it is quite easy to see that they all have a similar connecting idea. That idea is not calling anything by a name, but of giving something the distinguishing qualities or characters—which is the reason why anything gets a particular name. Thus *îkkerâ* is rendered as: "He (Adam, universal mind) *assigned* for name."

HIEROGLYPHIC INTERPRETATION
OF THE VERB *ÎKKERÂ*

Hieroglyphically, *îkkerâ* is rendered as: "He (Adam, universal mind) put into subjection or caused a state of latency to overtake his new emanation (faculty) so that the emanation was for a time unable to carry on its activities." A state of latency was necessary to designate (appoint) its distinguishing qualities and to develop in the emanation all ideas of conception, generation, and increase, literally as well as figuratively. This describes something that would grow, expand, rise, heap up, stack up, and pile up and then increase, inflate, and become huge and grand, so great in bulk as to suggest a mountain. It would bring fructification and production in great quantities. It would generate the elements of any progeny, any produce whatsoever. Finally, it would be the commencement or entrance into being.

The Hebrew words *æth sham-ô* reveal that the emanation was a definite, direct product of the universal mind (Adam) and that its distinguishing qualities could be seen exterior to the universal mind, rendering its name knowable. That is to say, the universal mind foresaw its new faculty in operation (what it could do), which enabled it to render its name as "Noah." So, what can Noah do?

NOAH

The Hebrew root from which this important name comes, is composed of the Hebrew sign of produced being (*N*), which is the image of reflected existence, and the sign of Nature's effort (*H*), which gives birth to vital equilibrium, to *existence*. The Hebrew and Chaldaic draw two verbs from the name *Noah*: NHOE, meaning "to lead to the end, to guide toward the place of repose," and NOUA, meaning "to repose, to rest tranquilly, to be in a state of peace, calm, or perfect bliss." The Hebrew text discloses that the name *Noah* is derived from the latter.

The text also discloses that *Noah* sees the end of the world and its renewal. That is, Noah is associated with the closing phases of Manvantara (period of activity or cycle of manifestation) and its renewal. This faculty's task is to bring into a state of vapor (by heating) or to sublimate all the fruits of the epoch—which are coming to an end—into the highest spiritual essence. Seeds and anything existing in possibility are thus preserved in a sublimated state during the period of repose (Pralaya), in which all forms are decomposed into integrant parts. In this state, their substance looses their characteristic vibratory frequencies, "returning to the quiescent, precreative state (stillness) symbolized by the waters in flood legends" (Geoffrey Hodson, *Hidden Wisdom in the Holy Bible Volume 2*, 52).

Noah is the emblem of the repose of elementary existence, the sleep of Nature, which is motionless, still, and not agitated. When Pralaya ends, *Noah* enables the universal mind to condense the potentialities and seeds once sublimated and "the great pilgrimage of involution and evolution is then repeated on a higher round of the ascending spiral" (ibid.). That is to say, when Pralaya ends, Manvantara is renewed.

HIEROGLYPHIC MEANING OF THE NAME *NOAH*

Further examination of the name *Noah* yields greater understanding. The radical vocabulary (a series of Hebraic roots furnished by THTR) discloses that the character *N* (first letter of the name *Noah*) is symbolic of every produced being, i.e., anything that is given a definite existence, a being, a personality, or individuality. Placed at the beginning of words, *N* expresses passive action folded within itself. It is not acting but is receiving impressions from external agents. It is the object of action rather than the subject and is in passive submission to divine laws.

N is the image of the reflected existence (a likeness of the source of existence). Consider this illustration. When light falls upon our planet, it is either reemitted or absorbed and turned into heat. When the reemitted light is returned into the medium from which it came, it is reflected. Simply put, we say that we see physical existence (creation) by the light it reflects; we see its images. *N* represents the images of the reflected existence (made of material substance), of the produced and reflected being, and of individual and corporeal existence.

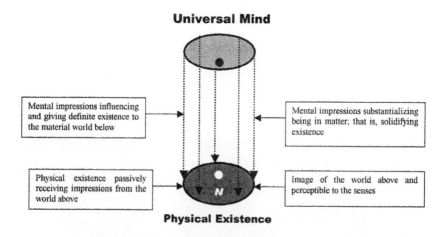

N: IMAGE OF THE REFLECTED EXISTENCE

Figure 28.1 above depicts *N*—image of the reflected existence— receiving mental impressions from the universal mind and influencing material activity.

The universal convertible sign *O* (second letter of the name Noah) is the image of the bond that binds *nothingness* (nonbeing) to *being* (existing in a certain state), which communicates from one nature (the mind) to another (matter, or material substance).

O: THE UNIVERSAL CONVERTIBLE SIGN

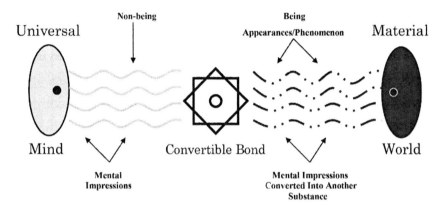

Figure 28.2 above depicts the convertible sign *O* communicating or converting mental impressions emanating from the universal mind into appearances (outward aspect of thoughts).

The convertible sign *O* joined to that of produced existence (*N*) produces a root whose vague and indeterminate sense is fixed only by means of the terminative sign by which it is accompanied. In this case, the sign *H* (*hêth*) terminates the name *Noah*. Therefore, *H* (*hêth*) fixes the meaning of this name. The radical vocabulary tells us that *H* (*hêth*) is the symbol of *elementary existence*. Webster's dictionary states that, the word *elementary* pertains to elements. It means, "initial, first principle, natural, primary, rudimental, simple, inchoate (existing in an elementary form)." The word *element* indicates one of the simplest constituent principles or parts of which anything consists, or upon which its constitution is based. It is an ingredient, as are the elements of which all matter is composed. For example, quartz, mica, and feldspar are elements of granite, and cells are the elements of living bodies.

Hence, *H* (*hêth*) united to the sign of "reflected existence" (*N*) signifies the elementary existence of the material world: *nature*—the natural processes or productions perceptible to the senses, as the physical characteristics of minerals, plants, and animals.

Further, Webster states that the word *existence* means "to come forth, to exist; life; sentient being; *continuance of real being* of anything that exists." The Kabbalah reveals that, that which continues real being is the universal mind (Adam). In other words, Noah enabled the universal mind to involute in matter the first elements or principles of physical, corporeal existence—mineral, plant, and animal.

CONTINUANCE OF REAL BEING

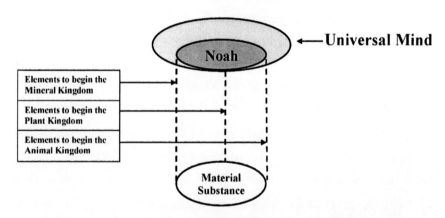

Figure 28.3 above shows the involution of elementary existence *H* (*hêth*) or of the first three principles in matter. It depicts Noah enabling the universal mind to animate material substance with the first constituent parts of the material world (mineral, plant, and animal). It is the starting point of elementary existence in the material world.

The sign *A* (third letter of the name Noah) signifies abstract principle, origin, beginning, potentialities, and first cause. In the midst of *H* (*hêth*) and the sign of reflected existence (*N*), the sign *A* signifies the starting point of elementary existence in the material world. Hence, Noah is an abstract principle or faculty that enabled the universal mind to substantialize (to give reality to) elementary existence in the physical world. That is to say, Noah, as a faculty operating within the universal mind, is the beginning source or operative cause of material existence.

Moreover, the sign *H* (*hêth*) discloses that elementary life— showing itself in activity, work, or striving of some kind—seeks an outlet, some means of expressing itself, some unrestrained, instinctive impulse to activity of some kind. Hence, *H* (*hêth*) is the sign of an effort of nature that gives birth to vital equilibrium and long-term stability. This denotes a state of poise or balance, reached after long-agitated elementary existence finds repose and remains firm. Therefore, nature is in repose: NOAH.

Long-term stability provided time for life to flourish and for complex animals and plants to evolve. It made Earth a hospitable planet.

ELEMENTARY EXISTENCE IN EQUILIBRIUM

The Hebrew word *l'æmor* reveals that every variation[1] and permutation[2] giving way to the impulsions of the universal mind were universalized when they demonstrated—or proved by invincible, conclusive evidence—the manifesting radiant movement or objectivity of existence proper in equilibrium. That is to say, when all forms, appearances, substances, positions, dimensions, properties, proportions, and possible changes in the arrangements of things were equilibrated, they were universalized (were made to pervade all).

The Hebrew words *înahome-nou* disclose that elementary existence in equilibrium yielded that perfect repose (*Noah*), which resulted from the *adamah*[3] (homogeneal ground) being agitated for a long time in opposite directions, and the point of equilibrium, which it attained where it dwelt immobile, thence, the repose of existence (*Noah*). This is likened to a state of rest produced when two forces acting upon a body are so opposed to each other that the body remains at rest—although one of those forces would move the body if it was acting alone—those forces are said to be in equilibrium; that is, they are equally balanced.

BRINGING SUBSISTENCE TO A MODERATE STATE

Înahome-nou further reveals that the faculty Noah enabled the universal mind to seize elementary existence, to cast down a compressive force upon it, and to envelop elementary existence (like a girdle shutting it in). Consequently, it heated and rendered elementary existence obscure, dark (the result of the envelopment).

In a broad sense, the general envelopment of elementary existence and the heat that resulted was an effect of the compressive force, which is to say, it was an effect of natural heat, solar fire, and torrefaction drying elementary existence by heat to reduce it to the state desired, and to condense it by the burnishing that followed.

NOAH'S GENERATIVE ARDOR

The word *generative* connotes having the power of producing or originating something. *Ardor* denotes a burning fire. As a symbol, fire may be described as a swift energy and penetrating power that cleanses and transforms dead matter into the likeness of its own leaping brightness. This symbolic meaning of fire and the significance of the word *generative* convey that the heat that resulted from the envelopment of elementary existence was the generative ardor of Noah enabling the universal mind to animate or bind nonbeing (dead matter) to being (existence). This conveys that within the universal mind Noah was the means to activate dead matter with organs (mediums) to act through and, therefore, to have existence.

The female principle within the universal mind was contributory. The Hebrew words *mi-mahoshenou* reveal that the female principle enabled the universal mind to aggrandize "existence," to tend to its entire development, and to serve as an instrument of generative power to manifest exteriorly the physical, low-down, and degraded sentient existence (the negative material polarity of Spirit). This carries the idea of an elementary existence that was made obvious. It had physical reality, superficies, and exterior forms, i.e., the mineral kingdom.

In addition, *mi-mahoshenou* reveals that growth and material development of sentient existence was assembled and conformed by the aggregation of elements, which was a consequence of an intelligent movement or plan formed in advance by the *will* (female principle) of the universal mind. Thence, growth and material development— which were once entirely vague and indeterminate (incomplete)— were now fixed, made stable, established, and equilibrated. That is, elementary existence reached *Noah.*

The Hebrew words *me-whitzebôn* and *îadeînou* elaborate on this growth and material development of matter.

GROWTH AND MATERIAL DEVELOPMENT
OF ESTABLISHED MATTER

Me-whitzebôn reveals that the element water (from which everything draws its nourishment) stimulated the growth and material development of determined matter. Determined matter was established substance endowed with physical properties. It fructified and produced spontaneously (without constraints). This conveys a movement of established matter—advancing, appearing evident, coming, and opening.

Îadeînou reveals that the spontaneous fructifications were the manifestation of potential faculties and every idea of power and of force arranged, prepared, and given agreeable forms. All manifestations of individual being that were shaped from the *adamah* (the homogeneal ground) and passed onto established matter fructified, without constraints, all accessory ideas of particularity (minuteness of detail), of individuality (distinct existences), and of property (inherent qualities). Water stimulated their growth.

ELEMENTARY SOUL OF NATURE: THE HIDDEN BEGINNING PRINCIPLE

The Hebrew word *asher* reveals that the hidden beginning principle of potential activity—power, force, and directed energy—was and is within the universal mind, which is to say that it is within the universal soul. To elucidate, let us refer to chapter 1 of this book under the literal meaning of the name *Adam*.

This section relates that Adam is "mind." The word *mind* is synonymous to the word *soul*, which has several meanings. Webster's dictionary describes *soul* as "the animating, the vital principle, the source of action, internal power, ardor, or spirit." To *animate* is "to make alive, to give life, to quicken, possessing animal life as the soul animates the body." *Vital principle* means "beginning, that from which anything proceeds, an operative cause." *Source of action* is "the origin of a moving force." *Internal power* is "an inward, interior force, that which moves the mind, a faculty." *Ardor* means "a burning fire, flame, and heat, as the ardor of the sun's rays. It is warmth, brilliancy." *Spirit* is "vigor, the breath of life; life itself; vital power, intelligence, vivacity; to excite, to rouse."

All these qualities of the soul compose the universal mind. Noah, as an extension of the universal mind, possesses these qualities. This conveys that Noah is used as a conduit to animate elementary existence. Noah, then, is the hidden beginning principle within the universal mind, an operative cause or faculty of potential activity vivifying elementary existence in the material world. This reveals that Noah is the *elementary soul of nature* enabling the universal to unfold the homogeneal ground, the *adamah* (from which the material world proceeds), which in this verse, we are told that *Ihoah*[4] (Yahweh) had cursed (*ærorha*).

The word *curse* is symbolic of limiting activities through divine laws and conditions imposed upon matter and upon the lower nature by moral law and by suffering, as evidenced, demonstrated, and determined in earthly existence.

ADAM'S MICROCOSM (10/10)

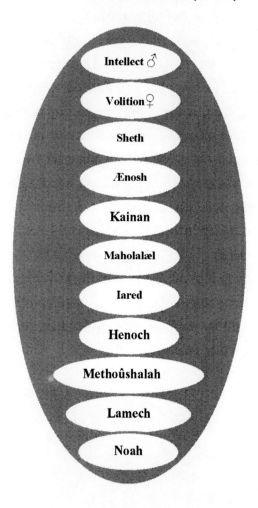

Figure 28.4 above depicts the addition of Noah to the unfolding faculties of the universal mind (Adam). The growing faculties of Adam within his microcosm are now composed of intellect (male principle), volition/will (female principle), Sheth (Adam's power to frame the foundation of the soul), Ænosh (Adam's physical faculties, corporeal man), Kainan (Adam's general invading force), Maholalæl (Adam's rising might and brightness), Iared (Adam's powers of steadfastness and perseverance), Henoch (Adam's corporate force

and panging qualities), Methoûshalah (Adam's "eager shaft of death), Lamech (Adam's ability to tie what tends to dissolution), and Noah (Adam's equilibratory force).

SUMMARY

Genesis 5:28–29 reveals that the universal mind emanated a new faculty and that assigning the name *Noah* to its new faculty distinguished its qualities. It reveals that as an emblem Noah symbolizes the repose of elementary existence, the sleep of Nature. Moreover, it reveals that within the universal mind, Noah is the hidden beginning principle of potential activity, power, force, and directing energy enabling it to unfold the homogeneal ground (the *adamah*)—from which matter was established—and which the Lord had cursed (put limitations on).

★ PRACTICAL APPLICATION

We learned in Genesis 5:28–29 that a state of rest is produced when two forces acting upon a body are so opposed to each other that the body remains at rest, in equilibrium, or equally balanced. This brings to mind two opposed forces, which ancient teachings tell us are always at work in the phenomenal world: positive forces and negative forces. The teachings reveal that these forces are always attracting each other, neutralizing effects. How then can we attract to ourselves the positive, the beautiful, without the interference of negative influences? Ancient teachings say it can be done, by tilting the balance.

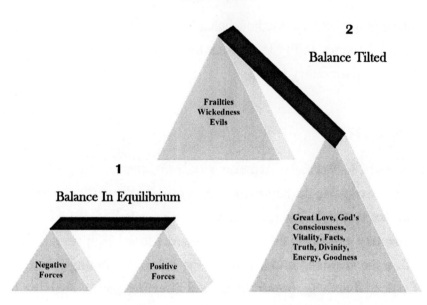

Figure 1 shows a scale with an equal amount of forces on each side. The balance is said to be in equilibrium. Figure 2 shows the balance tilted, owing to the greater weight on the positive side of the scale. In this example, tilting the balance was accomplished by adding good to good, positive to positive, godliness to godliness, and by becoming oblivious to the frailties of physical life, and its evils and wickedness on the other side of the scale, for those are things of the opposite side; they are the negative side of existence with which the spiritually minded individual has no concern.

CRITICAL THINKING

1. Genesis 5:28–29 reveals that an emanation was brought forth, which the universal mind named *Noah*. What faculty enabled the universal mind to keep the elements of its new offspring together?

2. Why did the universal mind assign the name *Noah* to its new emanation?

3. Describe Noah.

4. As an emblem, Noah is considered the repose of _____ _____.

5. The universal mind animated cold, dead matter by fire. In Kabbalah teachings, this kind of fire is also known as the _____ _____ of the universal mind.

6. The generative ardor of the universal mind was its _____ _____.

7. Based on the knowledge gained in this chapter, how was the female principle of the universal mind instrumental?

8. What hidden beginning principle within the universal mind enabled it to unfold the homogeneal ground (the *adamah*)?

9. The Lord cursed the *adamah*. What does this mean?

(Answers in Appendix B)

---

1. Variation denotes the altering of forms, appearances, substances, positions, dimensions, properties, and proportions.

2. Permutation denotes any possible arrangement of things in groups and the changing or combining of any number of quantities.

3. *Adamah* is the element that *Ælohim* drew from the creative waters and caused to pass from principle to essence (substance). The *adamah* is the homogeneous element, the beginning substance of mind that *Ælohim* created in order to make the universal mind, Adam.

The Kabbalist F. J. Mayers states, "The word *Adamah* is the word *Adam* with the addition of the *H* final, denoting a *tendency* or a movement towards some thing." The word *adamah* itself has the root *DM*, which denotes *assimilation* or *likeness*. This same root, *DM*, vocalized by the vowel *A*, is the Hebrew word for *blood*: *dam*. In Hebrew thought, *blood* and *likeness* are always associated ideas. In the word *Adam*, the sign *A* is prefixed to the root *DM*. The sign *A* denotes the starting point, potentiality, or cause of anything, so etymologically the word *Adam* means "potential likeness" or "potential assimilation."

Examining the word *adamah* sign by sign, the following is also revealed: *A* is the starting point, potentiality, or cause of anything. *D* is abundance born of division; it is the sign of a divisible and divided nature. *M* is the collective sign, developing "being" in infinitive space—as far as its nature permits—or uniting by abstraction into one single being all those of the same kind. *H* is the tendency or direction in which something moves. This reveals that the *adamah*'s tendency or direction of movement is to unite into one single being (Adam) all those of the same kind.

At first glance, *DM* is universalized sympathy. It is a homogeneous thing formed by the affinity of similar parts and holding to the universal organization of being. In a broader sense, *DM* is that which is *identical*; in a more restricted sense, it is *blood*, the assimilative bond between soul and body, according to the profound thought of Moses. Within the *adamah*, then, is that which assimilates, becomes homogeneous, and mingles with another thing. Thence, the general idea of that which is no longer distinguishable, which ceases to be different, renounces its seity or individuality, and is identified with the whole—is calm, quiet, silent, and asleep.

4. *Ihoah* is the Eternal Facultative Being. It is the Being of beings.

29

THE TIE OF WHAT TENDS TO DISSOLUTION: SIMILITUDES OF LAMECH, PART 1

GENESIS 5:30

- Translation from the King James Version of the Bible: "And Lamech lived after he begat Noah five hundred ninety and five years and begat sons and daughters."
- The literal English translation as it appears in *The Hebraic Tongue Restored*: "And he lived, Lamech, after the causing him to beget a son, five and nine tens of revolving change, and five hundreds of revolution and he begat sons and daughters (many issued offspring)."
- Transliteration from *The Hebraic Tongue Restored*: "Wa-îhî Lamech âhoreî hôlîd-ô æth-ben, hamesh w-thishehîm shanah wa-hamesh mæôth shanah wa-îôled banîm w-banôth."

The following interpretation of Genesis 5:30 is spiritual in nature, not physical.

PROEM

In chapter 25 we learned that the universal mind brought forth Lamech, a faculty that enables souls to keep the memory of past

229

events from dissolving after they passed through transition (or death of their physical body).

In this chapter, Genesis 5:30 reveals how the universal mind produced similitudes of this faculty—the symbolical sons and daughters of Lamech. Having the same attributes as Lamech, its similitudes will have the ability to tie that, which tends toward dissolution. That which tends toward dissolution is all life experiences that accumulate in the causal body[1] while the soul is incarnated (clothed with flesh).

At transition, those experiences causing the soul to evolve will go into the subconscious mind where they will be kept from dissolving or going into oblivion. These experiences will serve as causes to mold future incarnations of the soul and influence future conduct of man.

The Hebrew words *îhî*, *âhoreî*, and *hôlid* given in this verse reveal how the similitudes began to be developed.

UNFOLDING LAMECH'S SIMILITUDES

Îhî makes known that the impulsions of the universal mind upon elementary existence rendered elements obvious. Rendering these elements enabled the universal mind to become conscious of its faculty Lamech furnishing the power to bind the elements.

Âhoreî reveals that the elements were compacted and centralized, that the antagonistic forces surrounding the elements were reconciled, and that centralization of the elements enabled the universal mind to manifest an effluvium or ethereal, spiritual emanations of Lamech's similitudes.

Hôlid conveys that the effluvium was evidence of the similitudes' potential life or power of being, which was made obvious as the universal mind passed the effluvium from one nature to another, in an eccentric movement designed to extend, rise, and unfold the emanations in all directions within its sphere of activity. It necessitated the universal mind to execute its power over the universal quaternary and over its new progeny (*Noah*) to actively produce every manifestation of generative action, which would result in the generation of Lamech's similitudes. The underlying meaning of the number 595 given in this verse recounts the above events and following activities in precise details.

UNDERLYING MEANING OF THE NUMBER 595

The Hebrew words *hamesh*, *thishehîm*, *hamesh*, and *mæôth* compose the number 595, and they have been interpreted separately to render the hidden meaning of this number knowable.

Hamesh (number five) reveals that the universal mind exerted great effort upon elementary existence (the creative waters) to manifest the necessary elements to build the similitudes. The formative faculty of the universal mind gave it the power to mobilize (accelerate) the creative waters in order to render the elements palpable and compact, subsequently, enabling it to draw them from their depth.

The passive and conditional casuality of the universal mind took place on contact with the elements. It gave the universal mind impressions or mental images on how to proceed to form the similitudes. Accordingly, the plastic power of the universal mind was employed to fashion the elements.

Thishehîm (number ninety) reveals that the elements were passed from one state to another and that they were influenced by the interaction existing between the universal mind and matter—that is, by the multiplying function that occurs in the world of mind and matter. This interaction denotes that the universal mind was fashioning the elements in substance. This was a violent movement that resulted in a sudden irruption of material development and accumulation. The elements were made to gravitate toward a general mass, which consolidated and pressed them together. This kept them in an entire state. *Hamesh* reveals that the formative faculty of the universal mind enabled it to bring the elements together into a mass and its plastic power to give the mass form.

Mœôth (number one hundred) conveys that these activities were transitional movements that led the universal mind to mutate repeatedly.

Shanah discloses that mutations caused changes in the nature, essence, qualities, and attributes of the universal mind and it altered it in form indicating the universal mind had begun to manifest the similitudes, either in the order of things, or in the order of time, relative to its diverse mutations.

BRINGING FORTH THE SIMILITUDES OF LAMECH

The Hebrew words *îôled banîm w-banôth* reveal that the universal mind issued many offspring resembling its faculty Lamech. These were emanations proceeding from potentiality in action. They were intelligible embodiments characterized by Lamech's circumscriptive extent. They were the sameness of Lamech created by the universal mind to endow the souls of men with the ability to arrest dissolution of their life experiences at the end of each involutionary cycle; that is, to enable souls to chain in sequence their human existences (incarnations) after passing through transition or the so-called death of their physical form.

SUMMARY

Genesis 5:30 reveals that the universal mind produced similitudes of its faculty Lamech. It reveals they were created to endow the souls of men with the ability to arrest dissolution of their life experiences at the end of each involutionary cycle.

★ *PRACTICAL APPLICATION*

In this chapter, we learned that our souls are endowed with the ability to tie all life experiences as they transit from one incarnation to the next. The Kabbalah teaches that this is important, because all experiences helping our soul to evolve serve as causes that mold our future incarnations and influence our future conduct. Therefore, it behooves us to endeavor to acquire as many experiences as possible—particularly those that help our soul evolve.

One way this can be accomplished is through study. Mystery schools offer thinking, inquiring men and women the opportunity to acquire knowledge, which, once applied, aids the soul in coming into its fullness of expression, just as sure as day follows night, it accelerates learning.

Another way may be to take the road of hard knocks. The individual learns experientially. Life tosses him up and down, side to side, in every way imaginable. He learns through pain and suffering and by enjoyment. His truths are derived from his own thoughts, from his own observation of things around him. He advances his soul but at a slower pace.

CRITICAL THINKING

1. Genesis 5:30 reveals how the emanation of Lamech's similitudes were brought forth. For what purpose were they created?
2. What do the impressions received from being in contact with elements tell the universal mind?
3. What is the underlying idea when the universal mind is altered in form?
4. The Bible states in Genesis 5:30 that Lamech begat "sons and daughters." What is the hidden meaning of the phrase "sons and daughters" in kabbalistic terms?

(Answers in Appendix B)

[1.] Refer to figure 7.2 in chapter 7.

30

THE TIE OF WHAT TENDS TO DISSOLUTION: SIMILITUDES OF LAMECH, PART 2

GENESIS 5:31

- Translation from the King James Version of the Bible: "And all the days of Lamech were seven hundred seventy and seven years and he died."
- The literal English translation as it appears in *The Hebraic Tongue Restored*: "And they were, all the days (periodical lights) of Lamech, seven and seven tens of revolving change and seven hundreds of revolution and he ceased."
- Transliteration from *The Hebraic Tongue Restored*: "Wa îhî chol îmeî Lamech shebah w-shibehîm shanah, w-shebah mæôth shanah wa-îamoth."

The following interpretation of Genesis 5:31 is spiritual in nature, not physical.

PROEM

In the previous chapter, we learned that the universal mind developed the similitudes of its faculty Lamech to endow the souls of men with the ability to tie the memory of their successive incarnations together.

In this chapter, Genesis 5:31 discloses their progression into matter and the successive change undergone by the universal mind after completing this period of activities.

The Hebrew word *îhî*[1] reveals that the similitudes were arranged, prepared, and given agreeable forms after the creative waters were accelerated. It conveys that elements were procured upon mobilizing the waters and that all the attributes of Lamech were conveyed into the elements from whence the similitudes were built. Vivifying the similitudes is next in the agenda. The underlying meaning of the number 777 given in this verse yields the particulars.

UNDERLYING MEANING OF THE NUMBER 777

The Hebrew words *shebah*, *shibehîm*, *shebah*, and *mæôth* compose the number 777. Each word has been fully examined to make plain its underlying meaning.

Attached to the name *shebah* (number seven) are all ideas of accomplishment and consummation of things. *Shebah* reveals that the universal mind accomplished what it intended—namely, to produce a real and evident existence of Lamech's similitudes.

Shibehîm (number seventy) tells us that the universal mind produced the similitudes upon conceiving their existence within the abyss of its unlimited, negative, feminine potentiality of mind. Its female principle was the force that impelled the universal mind to bring forth the similitudes whose growth had manifested universally. Its conception was consummated upon the similitudes entering matter. By entering matter, *shebah* reveals the similitudes' entire state (their qualities) was quickened and enlivened hastening their continuity.

In succession, the universal mind changed its mode of existence. *Mæôth* reveals that its recent activities were transitional movements that led to its transmutation.

TRANSMUTATION OF THE UNIVERSAL MIND

Transmutation denotes successive changes under natural laws (cause and effect). These changes were cyclic, and revolved around the recent period of activities, which once completed replaced the universal mind to its state of seity, the state from whence it had begun to move. *Shanah* reveals that the universal mind was not found at the end of this period of activities in the same state as when it emanated Lamech. The Hebrew word *íamoth* relates that the universal mind had transformed into a different way of being.

The successive change made the universal mind ready to do specific work that was certain to effect the purpose for which the similitudes of its faculty Lamech were created—namely, to be unfailing agents having the power to arrest dissolution of memory at the end of the souls' involutionary cycles, chaining in sequence their human existences.

SUMMARY

Genesis 5:31 gives an overview of how Lamech's similitudes were developed and how their manifestation brought the conception of the universal mind to pass. Further, it reveals how the universal mind transformed into a different way of being, a successive change that came after completing a period of activities.

★ *PRACTICAL APPLICATION*

We learned in this and in the previous chapter that ties were developed to bind the memories of each incarnation together when our soul passes through transition. How glorious it would be for us to remember previous incarnations as well as we remember events from this incarnation! Many people, however, cannot remember experiences from one day to the next, much less from distant pasts.

Ancient teachings tell us that unless there is a health condition associated with failing memory and a decline in cerebral functions, remembering recent and distant-past events may be accomplished. Physically speaking, one can, for example, clear mental fog and feed the brain with nutrients to help improve memory.

Deepak Chopra, MD, and Rudolph E. Tanzi, PhD, wrote about clearing mental fog in their book *Super Brain*: "To move a constricted, cramped brain from old conditioning, outworn beliefs, ritualized thinking, habit, inertia, fear, and low expectations, we must expand our awareness." They say that having a closed mind does not feel good. To combat the inner discomfort, they suggest that the first tactic should be to expand our awareness, have an open mind, and turn an emotional event into a set of rational steps to rise above the level of problems and into the level of solutions.

This advice seems reasonable and can certainly help rid the mind of clutter. Without clutter, the brain is given an opportunity to awaken dormant faculties, which in turn will enable us to consciously retain the knowledge of recent past events, ideas, or impressions.

Spiritually speaking, one can attune to the universal mind to help bring the distant past to conscious awareness. Ancient philosophies teach that we do not have to pass through transition in order to become aware of our past lives. We can, in fact, remember previous incarnations by application.

Via meditation, we can subdue ourselves into subjection, bringing our thoughts and feelings concerned with the inner consciousness of distant-past events to conscious awareness; such types of meditation can be learned by acquiring the knowledge from reputable mystery schools.

CRITICAL THINKING

1. Where was the existence of Lamech's similitudes first conceived?

2. As unfailing agents Lamech's similitudes have the power to arrest what?

(Answers in Appendix B)

[1.] I wish to bring to the reader's attention the Hebrew word *ihî,* or יהי (1), which begins Genesis 5:31. This word defers from the Hebrew word *ihî* יחי (2) used in previous verses.

(1) ה Hè   (2) ח Hê

Notice that the characters of the Hebrew sign *H* in these two words are written differently. The first one is the *hè* sign (ה), symbol of universal life. It is that which is animating and vivifying, and it expresses life and the abstract idea of being. The second is the *hêth* or *hê* sign (ח), symbol of elementary existence, and represents the principle of vital aspiration or inhaling life, the field of man, his labor, care, and fatigue. In Genesis 5:31 Moses used the sign ה in the midst of the Hebrew signs *i* or *yod* (י) to convey the ideas expressed above while in the previous chapters, the sign ח was used. This is why the meaning of *ihî,* given in this verse differs from the meaning given to this word in previous chapters.

31

THREE SONS OF NOAH: THE SELF-EXISTING OF WHAT IS LOFTY AND BRIGHT (SHEM); OF WHAT IS GLOOMY, CURVED, AND WARM (HAM); AND OF WHAT IS EXTENDED AND WIDE (JAPHETH)

GENESIS 5:32

- Translation from the King James Version of the Bible: "And Noah was five hundred years old and Noah begat Shem, Ham, and Japheth."
- The literal English translation as it appears in *The Hebraic Tongue Restored*: "And he was, Noah, (nature's rest) a son of five hundred fold of revolving change and he begat, he Noah, the selfsameness of Shem, of Ham, and of Japheth (that is to say, the self-existing of what is lofty and bright, of what is gloomy, curved and warm, and of what is extended and wide)."
- Transliteration from *The Hebraic Tongue Restored*: "Wa îhî Noah ben-hamesh mæôth shanah, wa-îôled Noah æth-Shem, æth-Ham w'æth-Japheth."

The interpretation of Genesis 5:32 is spiritual in nature, not physical.

PROEM

We learned in chapter 9 that the *Law of Periodicity* connotes having periods of recurrence, performing cycles in equal times, or things taking place at fixed intervals, such as the periodic production of faculties and their similitudes, as revealed throughout Genesis 5. Concordant with this law, Genesis 5:32 tells us that a new period of activity began for the universal mind. The emanations of Shem, Ham, and Japheth conform to this knowledge. These are three divine aspects of Noah. Symbolically, they represent Noah's three constituent principles (the developed or decomposed triad of that collective unity), and they are related one to the other in the same manner as the effect is related to its cause. Let us elaborate.

UNDERLYING MEANING OF THE NUMBER 500

The Hebrew names *hamesh* and *mæôth* given in this verse compose the number 500. Examination of these names reveals the beginning stages of building the three constituent principles of Noah, and the extent of their development.

Hamesh (number five) reveals that great force was exerted upon elementary existence to render the necessary elements to build the three emanations. These were contractile movements made upon elementary existence to make the elements palpable and compact enabling the universal mind to draw them from their depth.

Apprehending the elements produced heat. Heat was the result of the contractile movements animating or exciting the elements, which awakened them from sleep or repose and roused them into action. This was conducive to receiving impressions or mental images of how to produce the three emanations, which the passive and conditional casuality of the universal mind served to promote. In succession, the plastic power of the universal mind supplied the means to begin to fashion the elements into Shem, Ham, and Japheth.

Mæoth reveals that the emanations were developed to the extent of Noah's circumscription and the desire of the universal mind to extend, dilate, and manifest them exteriorly. Their development was a sympathetic and reciprocal movement in accord with divine laws, and it was a transition that led the universal mind to mutate repeatedly. *Shanah* reveals these mutations in turn changed its nature, essence, qualities, and attributes. These changes, which altered the universal mind in form, convey the forthcoming emanations of the three existences either in the order of things, or in the order of time, relative to the diverse mutations of the universal mind.

THREE CONSTITUENT PRINCIPLES OF NOAH: SHEM, HAM, AND JAPHETH

The Hebrew word *iôled* and the names *Shem*, *Ham*, and *Japheth* reveal that the universal mind emanated three principles—the sameness of Shem (that which is lofty and bright), of Ham (that which is curved, dark, and hot), and of Japheth (that which is wide and extended). The three principles being the developed, or decomposed triad of that collective unity named Noah.

SHEM

In Hebrew the name *Shem* is spelled *Shm* (םש). The sign of relative duration and movement *sh* (ש)—connected here with the sign of exterior action, *m* (ם), and used as a final collective sign—compose the root *Shm*, which carries the idea of that which is distinguished exteriorly by its elevation, splendor, and dignity. In its most restricted acceptance, *Shem* is the proper name of a thing, the particular designation of a remarkable place or remote time. It is the mark, the sign by which they are recognized, rendering them knowable. Renown, splendor, and glory are attached to them.

In its broadest acceptance, *Shem* is the ethereal space, the empyrean, the heavens, and even God, as designated in Hebrew, Samaritan, Chaldaic, or Syriac.

The Hebrew text expresses that it is extremely difficult to choose, among so many significations, that which is most consistent with this emanation. Nevertheless, one can, without erring, translate *Shem* as "the sublime, splendid, radiant, lofty, bright one."

Hieroglyphically, *Shem* is expressed as that part of Noah operating within the universal mind to bring subsistence into matter. That is to say, *Shem* is the power possessed by the universal mind that descends into the sphere of activity (1) to vivify or quicken the circumferential extent[1] and (2) to develop "real being" (actual existence) universally.

HAM

In Hebrew, the name *Ham* is spelled *Hm* (חם). On the whole, this name is the opposite of Shem. The sign *H* or *hêth* (ח), which constitutes it, recalls all ideas of effort, obstacle, fatigue, and travail. The root *Hm*—which results from its union with the sign of exterior action, *M* or *Mem* (ם), employed as collective—presents (1) a bending, a dejection (or casting down), or a thing that inclines toward the lower parts and (2) the heat that follows a sharp compression: the hidden fire of nature: the warmth that accompanies the rays of the sun, and the blackness that results from their action.

In its broadest sense, *Hm* represents the sun itself, which is considered to be the cause of heat and of torrefaction (dry heat).

The Hebrew text conveys the idea that when the name *Ham* is presented alone and in an absolute sense, it can, to a certain point, be taken in a good sense, since it expresses the effect of the sun upon inferior bodies. But if one only sees in it the opposite of Shem, it offers only sinister ideas. If Shem is the sublime and superior, Ham is the abased and inferior. If the former is the radiant, exalted, and infinite, the latter is the obscure (gloomy), the bending, and the limited.

Hieroglyphically, *Ham* is rendered as elementary existence demanding some sort of effort, care, and fatigue.

In general, *Ham* renders this existence manifest and obvious and it declares to the senses. Ham is that part of Noah that represents:

- its hit-hard force that dejects, throws, or casts down a compressive or condensing force that renders existence obscure (dark);
- its compressive force shortening or drawing "sentient being" into smaller dimensions, giving the notion of an obtuse force that curves (bends from a rectilinear direction), is hot, envelops in a smooth, swift motion, and renders obscure. It brings subsistence to a proper degree of hardness;
- the natural heat, solar fire, torrefaction and the burnishing that follows a heated (condensed) existence;
- its generative ardor animating matter; and
- its power to generate, produce, or originate a burning fire that energizes and transforms matter—a fire that lays hold upon cold, dead matter and makes it sparkle and blaze, turning it into the likeness of its own leaping brightness.

JAPHETH

This name holds a sort of medium position between Shem and Ham. It partakes of their good or evil qualities without having them in itself.

In a generic sense, Japheth signifies material extent—the space or degree to which material existence is extended, its distance, quantity, and size. Japheth is that part of Noah that keeps subsistence within reasonable bounds.

In a more restricted sense, Japheth signifies latitude or breadth, width, and extent—the measure of material existence from side to side or at right angles to the length.

Japheth is spelled *Jphth* (יפת) in Hebrew. The root *phth* (פת), from which the name *Japheth* comes, contains every idea of:

- expanding (spreading), extending (stretching out in any direction), and allowing itself to be penetrated (entered or pierced). That is, Japheth facilitates expansion, extension, and penetration.
- solution, divisibility, and simplification. In other words, Japheth is capable of disentangling anything intricate, difficult, or mysterious, of separating or disuniting parts of bodies, of making things simple, of reducing to simplicity or singleness, of being unmixed or uncompounded and consisting of few parts.

In a moral sense, Japheth signifies:

- Freedom from duplicity or doubleness of heart or speech—that is, freedom from exhibiting different or contrary conducts or uttering different or contrary sentiments at different times in relation to the same thing
- Freedom from double-dealing or deceitful practices—where one professes one thing and practices another

- Freedom from simulation or hypocrisy
- Sincerity and honesty of mind or intention
- Truthfulness, genuineness, and earnestness
- Plainness—that is, being open, clear, uninterrupted by anything, not liable to be mistaken or missed, evident or clear to the understanding, obvious, not obscure, and not liable to be misunderstood; rough, unvarnished, free from difficulties or intricacies, simple, artless, and free from show, disguise, cunning, or affection (evil propensity as vile affections); open and frank

Moreover, Japheth is governed by the sign of potential manifestation, Yod (י), which adds to its moral force and universalizes it. This adds to Japheth's strength, and it becomes all-embracing, total, unlimited, boundless, comprehensive, entire, general, whole, exhaustive, and complete. By its nature, Japheth is fit to be predicated *of* many and has the fitness or capacity to be *in* many.

Hieroglyphically, Japheth (יפת) signifies the potential faculty of mind called *apprehension* or *comprehension*, which seizes through the understanding all ideas of beauty, grace, charm, and attraction, symbolically represented by the mouth of man, whose most beautiful attribute it depicts, is that of uttering his thoughts.

The Hebrew text discloses that Japheth emphasizes things one wishes to distinguish by speech, eloquence, or the power to express strong emotions in a vivid and appropriate manner, in oratorical inspiration, or by speaking with emphasis and making noticeable every idea of dilation. This extends the mind easily and allows one to penetrate, open, and affect the mind. It causes one to feel and to be moved deeply by reaching with the intellect to understand and grasp the hidden meanings of things, making way intellectually.

UNITY OF SHEM, HAM, AND JAPHETH

Shem, Ham, and Japheth are related one to the other, in the same manner as the effect (the three constituent principles) is related to its cause (Noah).

Containing all ideas of effort, obstacle, fatigue, travail, and exterior action, Ham represents phases of Manvantara (periods of activity; cycles of manifestation): (1) elementary existence in equilibrium, (2) the generative ardor of Noah operating within the universal mind to animate or bind non-being (dead matter) to being (existence), and (3) the growth and material development of the physical, low-down, and degraded sentient existence made stable, established, equilibrated. This coincides with the meaning of the sign *H*, the fourth letter in the name Noah.

Japheth signifies every produced being, anything given a definite existence, material extent, all fruits of the epoch and potentialities. This signification coincides with the meaning of the sign *N*, the first letter in the name Noah.

When all fruits and potentialities cease to come forth, at the end of a particular Manvantara, Shem sublimates them. Shem is a very powerful principle coinciding with the meaning of the sign *A*, the third letter in the name Noah. Being self-existing of what is lofty and bright Shem is that part of Noah that sublimates all fruits of the epoch—which are coming to an end—into the highest spiritual essence. All forms decompose into integrant parts and their substance looses their characteristic vibratory frequencies, returning to the quiescent, precreative state. Shem preserves their seeds and potentialities in a sublimated state during the period of repose (Pralaya). When Pralaya ends, Ham condenses the potentialities and seeds once sublimated and involution and evolution is repeated on a higher round of the ascending spiral. Manvantara is renewed. (Refer to the meaning of Noah in Chapter 28)

The sign *O*, the second letter in the name Noah, is the convertible bond between Ham (potentiality in action) and Japheth (produced existence). It conveys activity-manifesting existence.

Fabre d'Olivet states that, "It is possible with all the etymological light thrown upon Shem, Ham, and Japheth, that the reader may still find many obscurities in the hieroglyphic sense of their names; but if the reader is sincerely earnest in penetrating these ancient mysteries, toward which Moses has traced sure routes, although ignorance and prejudice even more than time, have covered them with obstacles, he must not become discouraged." (*Cosmogony of Moses*, THTR, 171)

SUMMARY

Genesis 5:32 reveals the emanation of Shem, Ham, and Japheth, the decomposed triad of that collective unity called Noah. Shem is the self-existing of what is lofty and bright. Ham is the opposite of Shem. Japheth holds a sort of medium position between Shem and Ham.

★ PRACTICAL APPLICATION

In this chapter the three constituent principles of Noah (aspects of the universal mind) were disclosed:

- elevation, splendor, and dignity (Shem)
- bending, dejection, and inclination toward lower areas (Ham)
- expansion, penetration, solution, and simplification (Japheth)

Symbolically, Shem is the meditative life, which delights in things concealed and regards love and holiness with utmost esteem. This is consistent with the most restricted and broadest acceptance of Shem.

Ham is the doctrinal life occupied with truth—without discerning or getting the strength from it. It is a form of life that—though growing out of the reformed mind—is nigh to evil and must be brought into permanent subjection. This coincides with the sinister ideas that Ham presents in comparison to the sublime and superior ideas that Shem presents.

Japheth is the active life that has the qualities that moral law requires, but it deals more with outward things of the material or phenomenal world. This coincides with the moral and hieroglyphic meanings of Japheth.

In rank, Shem stands first, but in their unfoldment, Japheth and Ham are developed before Shem. This reveals what is, in fact, ascertained by all experience: that the highest life in us is the last to develop.

CRITICAL THINKING

1. Possessing the faculty Noah enabled the universal mind to beget three divine principles. Name them.
2. How is Shem portrayed?
3. How is Ham portrayed?
4. How is Japheth portrayed?

(Answers in Appendix B)

---

1. Circumferential extent is also known as the material world.

EPILOGUE

The light thrown by this book belongs to a higher plane of thought. On this high plane of thought, the interpretation of the verses portrayed in this book is beyond the reach of all controversies regarding their meaning. When the underlying meaning of the name *Adam* (universal mind) and its progenies is apprehended, there is no room for skepticism on the subject.

The progenies are the lineage of the universal mind (Adam). They are its faculties, the so-called patriarchs of Genesis. They symbolize consecutive degrees of growth in the evolution of consciousness, within which rest the several faculties and virtues that are developed and realized by the universal mind, and subsequently, endowed to the souls of men to gradually build them up until finally, they are ensheathed in their vestures.

The lives of the progenies signify the periods in which a continued course was completed and the same course was repeated until all faculties and their similitudes were brought forth. The names of the progenies serve to link the consecutive effects (ascertained by the use of numbers) with their antecedent spiritual causes. They symbolize the gradual progression of the *universal mind*, from which its succeeding state was derived. In other words, chapter 5 of the Genesis account is concerned with the extension of the *inner states* of the universal mind through successive emanations.

The universal mind brought forth nine emanations. Sheth was the first emanation. The second was Ænosh (Enoch); the third was Kainan (Cainan); the fourth was Maholalæl (Mahaleel); the fifth

251

was Iared (Jared); the sixth was Henoch (Enoc); the seventh was Methoûshalah (Methuselah); the eighth was Lamech; and the ninth was Noah.

The nine emanations are all faculties of the universal mind. These faculties are bestowed upon man to enable him to evolve and to reach those stages of deliverance that are incorporeal and pass beyond phenomena.

As an underlying principle, *Sheth* enables the soul to gather within its "causal body" the efforts of its personality while incarnated. This gathering of efforts molds future lives and influences man's future conduct.

As the physical faculties of corporeal man, *Ænosh* enables man to come into contact with his inherent weaknesses, strengths, virtues, and vices to gradually bring him to a greater degree of unfoldment while his consciousness marches toward the divine.

As a directing force, *Kainan* serves to manifest all particular endowments of the soul in the material world.

As a rising might and brightness faculty, *Maholalæl* provides man with the ability to aggrandize and develop his being in its entirety— physically, mentally, morally, spiritually.

As the steadfast and persevering faculty, *Iared* provides the soul with the ability to involute its qualities into matter and to ascend them from matter (via evolution) with enhanced powers and virtues gained from the soul's experiences while encased in matter; a cycle that is repeated over and over until the Lesser Day when the soul is liberated from the Wheel of Necessity.

As a corporate force and panging qualities, *Henoch* provides moral precepts vital to man's spiritual unfoldment.

As the "eager shaft of death," *Methoûshalah* enables the soul to swiftly hurtle to the tranquil and happy existence after passing though transition.

As the tie of what tends to dissolution, *Lamech* enables the soul to fasten the memory of each incarnation in the subconscious mind after it passes through transition (the so-called death of the physical body). It supplies man with the power to remember or recollect things that continue to exist in the mind exempted from oblivion.

Noah serves to clothe all the other faculties with a physical vehicle of consciousness or "ark."

Edna E. Craven, DC, CTN, BCI

APPENDIX A
SYMBOLIC WRITINGS

NUMBERS

The real significance of numbers dates back to ancient literature. Numbers were employed in a system of symbolism to refer to something beyond enumeration alone.

Numbers can be used as symbols, because the universe is established upon quantitative relations that are repeated proportionally through different phases and divisions of the material nature of the universe.[1]

Being the foundation upon which all things are built, numbers are common to all planes of consciousness. They signify events, actions, things, deeds, and a portion or part. They are frequencies or vibrations from which all substances are made, and they denote qualities or characteristic attributes in things. In other words, numbers have certain powers that rest in an esoteric connection that exists between the relations of things and the principles in nature of which they are the expressions.

All numbers are represented by ten symbols, beginning with zero and ending with nine. In *The Hebraic Tongue Restored* by Fabre d'Olivet, the general signification of the Hebraic decade (one to ten) is given and applied to the first ten chapters of Genesis ("Cosmogony of Moses," 306).

Number 1 indicates principiation (the beginning or analysis into constituent or elemental parts) and stability. Here, the power of being appears in germ—the origin or principle from which anything proceeds, the rudimentary or first element from which development takes place. It is the constituent part, a primordial substance (first in order, existing from the beginning) and the vital source or necessary first cause that gives rise to principiation.

Number 2 is distinction (separating, distinguishing, and dividing) and transition. The principle here passes from power into action, as the germ is being acted upon.

Number 3 is extraction and liberation. Extraction, a consequence of division, becomes a kind of relative unity. This new unity is represented in a great many words under the idea of peace, welfare, perfection, eternal happiness, etc.

Number 4 is divisional multiplication where the whole is divided into parts. It is abundance born of division, i.e., the one becomes the many.

Number 5 is facultative comprehension, wherein faculties or powers are developed.

Number 6 is proportional measurement. It ascertains the extent, quantity, and dimensions (length, breadth, and thickness or depth) of things, which defined or reduces them to precision.

Number 7 is consummation and return. Seven is the number of complete restitution, of cyclic fullness. It expresses the idea of return to the place from which one has departed.

Number 8 is accumulation; the divided forms returning to their common principles and becoming united.

Number 9 is cementation and restoration consolidated, wherein new movement begins.

Number 10 is the aggregative and reforming power, or formative energy, whereby the natural forces unfold and act. This is the congregation of power, the elementary motivating force. It is every formation by aggregation. It makes, directs, and governs every motivating principle that incites to action or causes motion.

NAMES

Just as numbers are used to express events, actions, and things, names are employed to connect stages of development. They symbolize the distinction of qualities. Qualities are enjoined to identify themselves in all their ideas and activities with their spiritual distinctions denoted by names.

Thus, the names given to the patriarchs of Genesis in chapter 5 represent the distinguishing qualities being developed by the universal mind. These distinguishing qualities are the reason why they got their peculiar names: Sheth, Ænosh, Keînan, Maholalæl, Iared, Henoch, Methoûshalah, Lamech, and Noah.

---

[i] Partitions or divisions of the material nature of the universe, also known as planes of existence, are substance or matter of the general system of things. They are ranked according to the rates of vibration of the atoms in each division. In the current cycle of life, five divisions are actively involved in manifesting creation, and they are regarded as occupying the same space in the universe, one division inside the other.

DIVISIONS OF THE MATERIAL
NATURE OF THE UNIVERSE

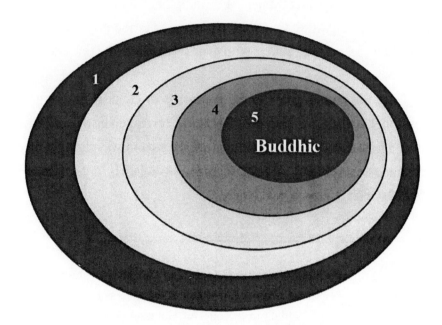

ONE PLANE WITHIN THE OTHER

The above figure depicts the five divisions of the material nature of the universe: (1) the physical plane, which is the material world, (2) the astral plane, which is the medium of the desires of the lower nature, (3) the emotional plane, which is the medium of the will/volition, (4) the mental plane, which is the medium of divine manifestation, where the creation of forms takes place, and (5) the buddhic plane, the innermost of all the planes, where the prototypes or patterns of things in the material world abide.

APPENDIX B:
ANSWERS TO "CRITICAL THINKING" QUESTIONS

CHAPTER 1

1. Three: literal, figurative, and hieroglyphic
2. The word *abstractly* means that the kingdom of man is separately and absolutely in a state or manner unconnected, unlinked to any other kingdom in nature (mineral, plant, or animal)
3. This knowledge tells us that "Adam" is to be a "group soul," a "living creature" for all souls or minds
4. The assimilative qualities of the Adam made him the perfect prototype (original model) and source of all the souls of humanity
5. Because Adam was made of the same character—essentially like and of the same or nearly the same nature—as Ælohîm. As a resemblance of Ælohîm, Adam was made of homogeneous indestructible parts.
6. This means that the mind becomes numerous by subdivision— that is, the one mind (Adam) becomes the assemblage of all minds (humanity)
7. Man is part of the universal mind. As such, man's mind has the same qualities as his maker
8. Faculties

CHAPTER 2

1. No
2. Intellect and will
3. It gives the mind an independent individuality and leaves it free to manifest itself in other and particular conceptions
4. *Intellect* serves as an instrument to receive or comprehend ideas communicated by the senses or by perception. *Will* serves as the principiant volitive faculty. It impels the mind to act on its conceptions
5. The female principle
6. The volitive faculty is the dynamo that feeds all the other faculties of the mind. It initiates and keeps in continuous operation all activities of the mind
7. Yes
8. The attraction and union of these two polarities keep the mind active and in motion. They are the forces of all creative activities, the relation of contraries in nature (creation), and the polarities upon which all-creative activities and manifestations depend
9. The male principle
10. The female principle

CHAPTER 3

1. Sheth, the foundation of the soul
2. Numbers
3. (a) The intellectual expansion of the universal mind, (b) a movement of extraction, (c) amalgamation, (d) creation of an existence, and (e) the development of the new existence
4. Sheth

5. Because of the faculty's distinguishing qualities

6. All the Truth inherited from the consciousness of Ælohîm and its ability to provide the foundation for the perceptible qualities of the soul to inhere

7. The mental, emotional, astral, and physical vestments, which are vehicles of consciousness in which the soul functions on the several planes of existence (mental, emotional, astral, and physical)

CHAPTER 4

1. This number reveals intrinsic processes involving the energetic, forceful, qualitative, and formative aspects of the universal mind to bring forth the souls of men. It also reveals that the souls of men bear the resemblance of the universal mind in structure

2. The universal mind became numerous by subdivision

3. As a microcosm of the universal mind

4. It can help man control the body in its important functions, aid man in answering important questions at crucial moments, and supply man with essential knowledge necessary to guide him aright in life

5. By attuning to or coming into communion with the universal mind

CHAPTER 5

1. Having produced a faculty to help build the groundwork of the soul, having produced the assemblage of souls, and having quickened the souls

2. The gradual process of consolidating the souls' loose constituent parts to preserve their individuality; the development of the souls; the development of their kingdom

3. By reflecting upon our conditions and searching diligently for the law upon which our being is established. This will help us to direct our energies with intelligence and to fashion our thoughts to fruitful issues

CHAPTER 6

1. In man's constitution
2. Man is endowed with life, can exist in a state of annihilation, and possesses strengths and weaknesses, virtues and vices
3. Ænosh
4. Corporeal man (physical faculties)
5. Because corporeal man changes and is capable of being altered in form, qualities, or nature.
6. Material substance
7. Being and nothingness, strengths and weaknesses, virtues and vices
8. Because he can be reduced to nothing and may have his identity, form, and distinctive properties destroyed through wars, self-destruction or suicide, murder, death, etc.
9. His strengths
10. His weaknesses
11. The higher virtues, the abstract mental virtues, and the lower virtues of the higher nature
12. Instabilities, caducities, and infirmities

CHAPTER 7

1. To serve as groundwork on which the various vehicles of consciousness of the souls can be built upon
2. The mental, emotional, astral, and physical vestures
3. Sphere
4. It involved extracting elements from elementary existence, followed by compressing and confining the elements from free movement to give them a definite form or expression that was compacted and centralized, and finally by unfolding the effluvium that arose from the centralized elements
5. Cognitional or causal body
6. Intellection associated with the organs of perception
7. The senses
8. The emotional vesture
9. The astral vesture
10. Solids, liquids, gaseous materials
11. The harsh, rigorous, exacting, inordinate, and vehement movements of the universal mind involuting the qualities of the foundations into matter
12. Forming models of its faculty Sheth

CHAPTER 8

1. Its will or female principle
2. To unfold and be acted upon by the aggregative, reforming power or formative energy of the universal mind
3. The gradual process of consolidating or pressing together the foundations' loose constituent parts to preserve their individuality from loss and keep them in an entire state

CHAPTER 9

1. Two were endowed: the male and female principles; and three were brought forth thus far: Sheth, Ænosh, and Kainan.
2. The production of a new faculty
3. The transformation of the universal mind into a different way of being
4. It mutates.
5. It changes its nature and essence and its qualities and attributes.
6. Its general invading force
7. Kainan
8. The universalization of its material development conveys the nature of Kainan has the capacity to be *in* the many
9. Means; material existence
10. All particular manifestations of individual being
11. In matter that is not yet formed but is suitable to be put into action; that is, it is suitable to produce or individualize existence proper

CHAPTER 10

1. The impulsions of the universal mind upon elementary existence to render elements manifest and obvious
2. The universal mind labored to keep the elements in equilibrium, even, uniform, in the same state, with likeness in dimensions, value, degree, and the like
3. To set and give the elements definite form or expression that was compacted and centralized
4. Centripetal and centrifugal forces

5. The universal mind acting upon the universal quaternary and upon its faculty Kainan, the medium through which the physical faculties would attain their material existence

6. Embryonic state

CHAPTER 11

1. Because these waters hold the elements of everything that is to exist

2. Mutation affected their boundaries, their designations, their dispositions, and their measures

3. It developed a medium to attain the material existence of all particular manifestations of the soul; it developed and endowed the similitudes of Ænôsh to the souls thereby given them the ability to take to the circumference (the material world) the physical faculties of corporeal man and its instabilities, caducities, and infirmities all of which were designed to gradually bring the souls of men to a greater degree of unfoldment

CHAPTER 12

1. Maholalæl

2. To give the souls of men a strong potential for exaltation, greatness, dignity, splendor, and glory

3. The employment of the invading and compressive power of the universal mind (Kainan) upon unformed matter

4. In the unlimited, negative, feminine potentiality of the universal mind

5. To activate the female principle

6. Its female principle

CHAPTER 13

1. Mediums are vehicles of consciousness used by the souls to function in the mental, emotional, astral, and physical planes of existence
2. Mumia
3. Vaccine, a vehicle of a semi-astral virus; nerves, conduits of sensations; and blood vessels, conduits of blood
4. Vital energy; organic, inorganic
5. The mediums of consciousness were made in the image of Kainan
6. Centralization served to identify the elements as being the ones to produce the intended effect
7. The increase in volume is expressed by the adverbial relations *much, more, still more,* and *many*
8. Numbers

CHAPTER 14

1. Number ten signifies the aggregative and reforming power (formative energy) of the universal mind, as well as its congregation of power proper
2. The power of the number ten
3. Evolving
4. The Law of Continuity and Reciprocity
5. The Law of Cause and Effect

CHAPTER 15

1. Steadfastness and perseverance
2. The universal mind is firmly fixed or established; it is constant and resolute, not fickle or wavering.
3. The universal mind continues in a given course without giving up
4. Good: to ascend with enhanced powers and virtues; evil: to sink, to descend into matter
5. Iared
6. They begin to manifest as an effluvium—or fluidic, ethereal, spirituous emanation—that unfolds by effect of a steady, indefinite movement of the soul.
7. Powers and virtues
8. The soul; form
9. All qualities and potencies of the soul
10. Its physical form

CHAPTER 16

1. The universal mind became conscious of its faculty Maholalæl serving as an instrument of generative power to manifest exteriorly the similitudes of this faculty and all the notions attached to its identity
2. Centripetal and centrifugal forces
3. It enabled the universal mind to direct the spiritual emanations of Maholalæl's similitudes downward into the sphere of activity
4. The furthest point to be reached in the polarization of mind and matter

5. The universal mind must mobilize the creative waters where the elements of anything that is to exist are held in solution
6. Circumscribe; attributes
7. Rise up; shine

CHAPTER 17

1. Metamorphosing the elements of Maholalæl's similitudes into a consolidated state to preserve them from loss and keep them in an entire state
2. Because the universal mind had grown in stature by producing Iared and by developing Maholalæl's similitudes

CHAPTER 18

1. Henoch
2. To solidify the assimilative, reflective, and transient life of corporeal man, and to give redemption to corporeal man through repentance and contrition
3. The universal mind became conscious that possessing its faculty Iared enabled it to move elements downward into the sphere of activity
4. Universal mind must mutate universally and ontologically, thereby changing its nature, essence, qualities, and attributes, and it must alter in form
5. Repentance and contrition
6. Corporeal man
7. Repentance and contrition

CHAPTER 19

1. To help involve the souls' potential qualities in matter so they can evolve from matter with enhanced powers and virtues
2. (1) The power to persist in anything undertaken upward through evolution, (2) the power to persist downward through involution, (3) the power to persist in governing, predominating over, influencing most prominently, having the greatest effect upon, giving specific character or appearance to, and overshadowing while the soul is encased in a transitory form—that is, while the soul is inhabiting its physical vehicle of expression

CHAPTER 20

1. It accelerated the movements of the waters to manifest the elements necessary to render Iared's similitudes
2. It transformed into a different way of being
3. The Law of Cause and Effect

CHAPTER 21

1. Methoûshalah. Its purpose is to hurl souls upward toward the eternity of existence after passing through transition, or the so-called death. It quickly moves souls to that which is tranquil, happy, orderly, and in the way of salvation (preservation from destruction)
2. Two kinds
3. The gulf or abyss of death precipitates, hastens without preparation, or throws headlong from a height—devouring, destroying, and consuming wantonly and with violence.

4. Death

5. The "dart of death"

6. Symbolically, Methoûshalah represents the soul being passed from one nature to another on the ascending curved line of the sphere of activity to that which is tranquil, happy, orderly, and in the way of salvation or preservation from destruction

CHAPTER 22

1. To be carried in every sense, to go to and to come

2. Commandments

3. Authoritative rules of action

4. Moral conduct, laws, instructions, injunctions, and maxims

5. To instill the precepts of God in the myriad of souls that would eventually become humanity

6. HE-They-who-are: the Being of beings; the unity of the Gods

7. Henoch is the moral sense and is necessary for the progressing, upward life movement of the soul

CHAPTER 23

1. Elements (electrons, protons, and other constituent parts) to build Henoch's similitudes

2. The universal mind had grown in stature from having reproduced and developed its corporate force and panging qualities, and from having produced its "eager shaft of death," Methoûshalah

CHAPTER 24

1. To scrutinize or observe closely the temper, character, nature, or tendency of this faculty, whether intellectual, moral, or emotional
2. Because Henoch had transmuted in its mode of existence. Henoch had become insubstantial
3. Vital power

CHAPTER 25

1. Lamech
2. (1) As a "knot," Lamech ties that which tends toward dissolution; and (2) as the "pliant bond," Lamech binds each incarnation like a chain to hold the memory of past lives together
3. It means this movement is directed toward the universalization of a considerable number of men (minds) united by a common bond (the universal mind)

CHAPTER 26

1. To provide the souls of men with the power to swiftly hurtle toward the eternity of existence upon transition

CHAPTER 27

1. Quickened; evident existence
2. The Law of Cause and Effect

CHAPTER 28

1. Lamech
2. To distinguish its character or qualities
3. Noah denotes all ideas of conception, generation, and increase. It brings fructification and production in great quantities. It generates the elements of any progeny, any produce whatsoever. It is the commencement or entrance into being (existence)
4. Elementary existence
5. Generative ardor
6. Faculty Noah
7. The female principle served as an instrument of generative power to manifest exteriorly the physical, low-down, and degraded sentient existence
8. Noah
9. The Lord put limitations to the activities of the lower nature through moral law and through suffering

CHAPTER 29

1. To tie in sequence all life experiences (incarnations) of the soul
2. Impressions give the universal mind images of how to form its faculties and the similitudes of its faculties
3. Altering in form carries the idea that the universal mind is manifesting a new existence. In Genesis 5:30, this new existence is the similitudes of Lamech
4. Sons and daughters are similitudes of the universal mind's faculties. They were created to endow the souls of men with the same faculties (powers) that are needed for them to evolve

CHAPTER 30

1. Within the abyss of the unlimited, negative, feminine potentiality of the universal mind

2. As unfailing agents, Lamech's similitudes have the power to arrest dissolution of life experiences at the end of the souls' involutionary cycles

CHAPTER 31

1. Shem, Ham, Japheth

2. As the self-existing of what is lofty and bright

3. As a bending, a dejection, a thing that inclines toward the lower parts, the opposite of Shem. Seen as an effect of the sun upon inferior bodies, Ham can also be considered good

4. As holding an intermediary rank between Shem and Ham. Japheth signifies, in a generic sense, the material extent, space, or degree to which material existence is extended—its distance, quantity, and size. In a restricted sense, Japheth signifies latitude or breadth, width, and extent—the measure of material existence from side to side or at right angles to the length.

BIBLIOGRAPHY

Volumes quoted from or consulted in the preparation of a kabbalistic rendering of Genesis 5 and its practical applications.

Allen, James. *As a Man Thinketh*. Philadelphia: Running Press Book Publishers, 1989.

Batmanghelidj, MD, F. *Your Body's Many Cries for Water*, second edition. Falls Church, Va.: Global Health Solutions, Inc., 1995.

Chopra, MD, Deepak and Tanzi, PhD, Rudolph E. *Super Brain*. New York: Harmony Books, 2012.

D'Olivet, Fabre (FD'O). *The Hebraic Tongue Restored*, trans. by N. L. Redfield. New York: Knickerbockers Press, 1921. Reprinted by Samuel Weiser, 1976.

Gaskell, G. A. (GAG). *Dictionary of All Scriptures and Myths*. New York: Lucis Publishing Co., 1930.

Gesenius, H. W. F. *Gesenius' Hebrew-Chaldee Lexicon to the Old Testament*. Grand Rapids, Mich.: Baker Books, 1979.

Hewitt, Paul G. *Conceptual Physics*, sixth edition. Glenview, Ill.: Scott, Foresman and Company, 1989.

Hall, Manly P. (MPH). *The Secret Teachings of All Ages*. Los Angeles: The Philosophical Research Society, Inc., 2000.

Hodson, Geoffrey (GH). *Hidden Wisdom in the Holy Bible*, *Vol. I and II*. Wheaton, Ill.: Quest Books, 1993.

Holy Bible King James Version. Nashville: Holman Bible Publishers, 1982.

Mayers, Fred J. (FJM). *The Unknown God.* Birmingham, England: Thomas's Publications Ltd., 1948.

Powell, Major Arthur E. *The Etheric Double and Allied Phenomena, 1925.* London: The Theosophical Publishing House Limited, 1925.

Strong, LLD, STD, James. *Strong's Exhaustive Concordance of the Bible.* Iowa Falls, IA: World Bible Publishers, 1986.

Webster, LLD, Noah. *New Twentieth Century Dictionary* (unabridged). New York: The Publishers Guild, 1946.

CPSIA information can be obtained at www.ICGtesting.com
Printed in the USA
LVOW06s0011170315

430787LV00001B/4/P

9 781452 519456